AGAINST ALL ODDS

AGAINST ALL ODDS

The autobiography of Gary Mabbutt

by
GARY MABBUTT

With Harry Harris

COCKEREL BOOKS LTD

Published by Cockerel Books Ltd
23-25 Maddox Street
London W1R 9LE

ISBN 1 869914 11 2

Jacket designed by Stephen Knowlden Associates
Jacket Photos by (*front*) Action Images (*back*) Bob Thomas

Photoset in North Wales by
Derek Doyle & Associates, Mold, Clwyd
Printed in Great Britain by
Butler & Tanner Ltd, Frome and London

To Philip Raymond Mabbutt

FOREWORD (1)

I think the word that best sums up Gary Mabbutt is commitment. Everyone knows how hard it is to get to the top as a professional footballer. What only a few people know – or perhaps not so few, since diabetes affects one person in a hundred in this country – is the commitment it takes to make a success of a life with diabetes. To combine top class football with diabetes takes a very special sort of person. Gary's performance on the football pitch has given pleasure to fans all over the world, but I wonder how many have paused to think of the very special meaning it holds for those, particularly the young, who themselves have diabetes. Gary has provided hope and inspiration for countless thousands by showing in the most practical way possible that if you can learn how to live with diabetes, the sky really is the limit.

I would not care to count the number of times I have turned to someone with diabetes and said 'if Gary Mabbutt can do it, so can you'. The message of this book is simple: you really can.

E.A.M. Gale MA, FRCP
Consultant in Diabetes
St Bartholomew's Hospital

7

FOREWORD (2)

There is no doubt in my mind that I have never come across any player like Gary Mabbutt.

Injury is an every day hazard for the professional footballer: diabetes is not. Any manager will tell you, there are certain players who use their injuries to escape responsibility. Because of it, some of them never reach their full potential – they simply will not deliver the goods when it matters. What do you say, then, about a 17-year-old who discovers he is diabetic but, instead of giving up, learns how to cope with it, gets back into training within two weeks, captains the England Youth Team, becomes a star with and captain of one of the country's top teams and goes on to represent his country at Under 21, 'B' and Full international levels? You have to say that he is something special and, as far as I am concerned, Gary Mabbutt certainly is.

His adaptability, his skills, his athleticism and work-rate would all be remarkable in a young man enjoying perfect health. In a lad who has to cope daily with the problems of a debilitating illness, these attributes are astounding. Yet, I have never known Gary Mabbutt to look for sympathy or make a fuss about his diabetes. The nearest he gets to advertising the fact is the bottle of Lucozade that he brings with him to every training session and places at the side of the pitch by the centre line. Also, from time to time, on a long flight, Gary will quietly get up from his seat, put on his jacket and stroll off to the toilet. Very few of his fellow passengers will realise that he has slipped quietly off to give himself one of the self-injections that he needs on a regular basis to keep his metabolism in balance.

The thought of it fills me with horror – Gary takes it calmly in his stride.

It is the same air of quiet authority which has brought him the captaincy of Spurs and which led me to pick him for my very first Wembley International, when I became England Manager in 1982. However, on top of his basic health problem, Gary is not immune to common or garden football injuries and, unfortunately, a groin strain subsequently put him out of the reckoning for three months, during which time other players had a chance to establish themselves.

I have not, therefore, been able to give Gary a regular run in the England Team, but he is a valuable squad member and is always in my mind for selection. He has never let me or his country down. There is one particular moment that sticks in my mind as being typical of Gary Mabbutt the player. We were playing Yugoslavia in one of the early qualifying matches for the 1988 European Championships. A difficult game. Yugoslavia were widely regarded by the commentators as the biggest threat to us in the group and, as is often the case at Wembley, we had had one or two shaky moments in the first quarter. Then we had a corner on the left. The ball came over and there was Gary, climbing impossibly high – it looked like 19 feet to me – and powering an unstoppable header into the back of the net. We did not look back after that, went on to win the match and, of course, the group.

I shall also always remember with gratitude the times when, on more than one occasion, I have suffered from the usual list of withdrawals from the England Squad and have called upon Gary at the last minute to help me out. His response is always immediate: 'I'll be right there Boss,' in that unmistakable West Country burr – although it did once take him a couple of hours because he had to find a babysitter for the dog! It is a thankless task to be called late into a Squad as cover and to have to sit through a big match without even getting your kit on. Whenever he has been asked, Gary has done this for me without complaint and has been delighted simply to be back on the scene.

10

· GARY MABBUTT ·

For me Gary is the original Bionic Man. I wish him every success with this book, which I am sure will prove an inspiration to many youngsters facing a setback in their lives, and with the rest of his career in football.

Bobby Robson
England Team Manager

September 1989

INTRODUCTION

This is the story of no ordinary footballer: Gary Mabbutt has defied all the odds.

To play for England and to captain Spurs is a feat in itself. To reach such sporting heights battling courageously against the affliction of diabetes is an amazing accomplishment.

I have assisted a number of top footballing personalities – players and managers – in the production of their life-stories. Many soccer stars' autobiographies are produced every year, but in my opinion few can compare with this story of the sheer will-power and determination exhibited by Gary Mabbutt.

Gary has been an inspiration to thousands of young boys and girls who have been told the hard-to-accept, and even harder-to-understand, news that they have diabetes. He has received something like 30 letters a week ever since he developed the condition at the age of 17.

This easy-going footballer has become the 'Marge Proops' for diabetes. Hundreds have written to him for advice, for help, for guidance, for comfort. He answers them all.

His message is simple. He is living proof that it is possible to be a diabetic and lead a normal life.

These days diabetes can be controlled and Gary knows all about that now. But he didn't know too much when it first struck him. He was bewildered, lost, helpless, confused. He knows that many kids in the same predicament feel the same way. He can help, and he does.

Besides all that, Gary is also a pleasant character, setting the right example with an exemplary disciplinary record, despite being a tough tackling player in an age when the image of the national sport has been brought into question by some unsavoury characters.

He is from the Trevor Brooking–Glenn Hoddle school of good conduct: an asset to be admired in an age of so much anti-social behaviour. Gary is the perfect model professional for youngsters to admire and copy.

He has earned the reputation of being one of the country's greatest ever utility players ... being dubbed 'Mr Versatility'. He has turned out at right-back, left-back, centre-back, centre midfield or wide in midfield or even in attack.

After one Wembley performance in an England shirt he was rightly praised as being an outstanding deputy for the England and Manchester United skipper Bryan Robson.

Bobby Robson, after watching him score twice – from left-back – for the Under 21s in Denmark, first coined the phrase 'the bionic man'. Immediately Robson elevated Mabbutt, after just a few months of his breakthrough from Bristol Rovers to the big time with Spurs, to the full international scene with a debut at Wembley against West Germany, when he was, quite remarkably, chosen to play in two positions!

Gary has played 13 times for his country and has been proud to do so. He has been involved in almost 30 full England squads.

His greatest disappointment was being left out of Robson's World Cup 22 for the 1986 finals in Mexico. There will always be a suspicion that, for once, Mabbutt's diabetes may have worked against him. Perhaps the England back-room staff suspected that the rigorous acclimatisation needed in Mexico might affect him. Certainly his ability and effectiveness with England at that time suggested that he would go to Mexico.

Again he was omitted from the 1988 European Championship squad in West Germany, despite contributing to England's successful series of qualification matches.

One of his claims to soccer fame is that he is the only man in the history of the FA Cup to have scored twice – once at each end. The 1987 FA Cup Final was the only cup final settled by an own goal, but, as Gary will tell you, it was 'the perfect fluke'.

The big consolation in his first, and so far only, FA Cup final came from the Duchess of Kent as she handed out the losers' medals to the Spurs team. She praised Gary for all his good work on behalf of diabetics.

Now Mabbutt, as skipper of a Spurs under the guidance of manager Terry Venables, and with a new-look £8 million team, will be pressing for his place back in the England squad to prove he is still the nation's No 1 utility player.

Even more significant than his footballing prowess, however, is the fact that he has been an inspiration to thousands of people, young and old, afflicted by diabetes. He has helped them by simply proving that a kid's dreams can still come true. You can play for England, diabetic or not.

Gary himself does not seek self-praise or glorification. He will not willingly admit the huge personal risks he has taken to prove to himself and to the youngsters he has helped that it is possible to lead a normal life – that it is possible to live *with* diabetes.

Harry Harris
Croydon
September 1989

CHAPTER ONE

'GARY, YOU'RE DIABETIC'

If there is one day that will haunt me for the rest of my life, it is the day I was diagnosed diabetic.

I was 17 years old, a professional footballer at Third Division Bristol Rovers and dreaming, like all youngsters, of one day playing for England. Suddenly it seemed my life had been completely shattered.

It was December 1978, a few days after the traumatic news that my father was leaving and our family was splitting up. I was due to play centre-half for Rovers at Leicester, but I had begun feeling very strange. In training I was constantly thirsty, gulping down liquid, always dashing to the toilet. Also, I was not sleeping very well at night.

The other players were kidding me no end about all this and the dressing room joke was that I had been drinking so much over Christmas that I couldn't stop.

But, joking apart, during that match at Filbert Street I felt the worst I ever have done during any game of football. At half-time I was downing cup after cup of water. To make matters worse, we lost badly and I didn't have a very good game. In fact, I was so bad that on the coach trip home the manager Harold Jarman, a former player with the club, had already decided to drop me for the next game.

He broke the news gently, explaining that after such a hiding he considered it better to leave me out for the following

Saturday ... our big FA Cup third round tie against first division Aston Villa. Not only was I feeling pretty ill, I was now feeling very low as well.

Next day in the local Bristol press I was condemned for my performance. When I picked up the newspaper there was a picture of myself staring back at me. The article said that I looked like a boy amongst men. My performance was torn to shreds – they told me how often I had been beaten to the ball, how I was to blame for one of the goals because I had lost possession. You can imagine how a young player feels after reading such comments. Devastated.

Still, it's no wonder people say that a week is a long time in soccer, because by the middle of that week I was back in the team! Because of a couple of injuries from the previous match I was now picked to face Villa in the FA Cup. For the first time for days I began to feel a little better.

I was looking forward to marking Brian Little and I really enjoyed the game. Although we actually lost 1-0 I felt I played well. In retrospect, it was probably the extra adrenalin of the occasion, the excitement of the Cup, the passion of a capacity crowd, that got me through it. The same paper that had been slagging me off the previous week, now praised me.

The Tuesday after the cup-tie we had a running session the length of the football pitch at our training ground at Eastville Park. I've always been a good trainer, always fairly sharp and fast, and certainly well up with the rest. That day I was 50 yards behind the others!

I couldn't believe it. More importantly, I couldn't understand it. The manager, quite rightly, wanted to know what was the matter with me. I told him I didn't know but that the previous week I had not been feeling at all well. He sent me straightaway to the doctor, whose practice was around the corner from the training ground.

He gave me urine and blood tests.

'Gary,' he said, 'you're a diabetic'.

It didn't really hit me that hard at first. I remember wondering what on earth a diabetic was, knowing something was wrong, that it was serious because the doctor told me so, but not having any idea how serious. I thought I might have been suffering from some sort of infection or virus and I certainly didn't expect to be sent straight to hospital.

The specialist came to see me. Sitting down beside my bed he started to explain what diabetes was and what it would mean to me for the rest of my life. He talked on about injections, insulin, food numbers, sugar levels in the blood ... but through it all there was really only one thing on my mind: would I be able to go on playing professional football?

Although he tried to sound optimistic, I could tell that the specialist was unsure of the answer to what was, for me, the most important question of all. At the time, of course, the subject of diabetes and professional sport was largely an unexplored one – unknown territory where there was very little to go on and very few who had gone before.

My dad contacted all the top specialists. A couple of them were adamant that I would not be able to play professional football, definitely not at the highest level. A couple of others thought I might be able to! Luckily the specialist in Bristol had heard of Danny McGrain's case – he had diabetes and still pursued his top level football career. That was all I needed to know, it made up my mind to play on. I was determined. Had every doctor felt I should have given up I would have done, but I was given some hope and I wanted to grab it ... with both hands. Nobody knew what was ahead of me, but at least the worrying three days of indecision, panic, fear were over and I knew what I wanted to do.

The local paper was following my case closely and they contacted Danny McGrain. Although I didn't get the opportunity to talk to him personally until a year later, his encouraging comments definitely helped me enormously. To hear from someone with the same problem who had decided to continue in football gave me another reason to give it a go myself. Danny and I keep in touch regularly now, comparing notes and seeing if we have any mutual problems. At the time, though, this didn't alter the fact that I had to come to terms with my diabetes myself … alone.

However, I decided when I was still in hospital that I would not keep my condition a secret. I was given a choice and felt that the best thing would be for as many people as possible to know about what had happened to me. It wasn't that I was particularly special, simply that I felt – and still feel – that the more that is known about diabetes, then the more people will understand. Perhaps diabetics will be encouraged to continue with what they want to do, rather than see insurmountable problems ahead for the rest of their lives.

I began to learn, and quickly, a great deal about diabetes with the help of the British Diabetic Association – and, if I say so myself, I'm now something of an expert on the subject! To try to explain it simply, briefly and unscientifically: a lot of what we eat turns to sugar naturally in the body, raising the level of sugar in the blood. The pancreas produces insulin, again naturally, to counter-balance this and keep the blood sugar level from going too high. If the pancreas starts functioning less well, or packs up completely, the blood sugar levels get higher and higher, dangerously so, and can result in death. To compensate for a malfunctioning pancreas, insulin can be injected into the blood to correct its sugar level. Before the discovery of insulin in 1921, if you suffered from pancreatic failure you faced certain death. Nowadays, you may have to learn how to give yourself injections, measure the sugar level in your blood, and know what's in the food you eat, but at least you have the chance to live.

When the doctor first told me that I would be injecting myself at least daily for the rest of my life I was appalled. I'd always hated the mere thought of an injection and now … to administer them to myself! Still, if it boils down to learning to give yourself injections or dying – well, what choice do you have? I was given an orange to practice on – to get the angles right. Actually, it didn't take as long as I thought it would and in only a matter of days I was injecting myself.

Apart from the injections, I had to learn all about food. Now I would have to weigh out all my meals and follow a strictly coordinated diet. And there would be no more sweet things like cokes, cakes or Christmas pudding. And the big box of Maltesers which my brother brought in for me in the hospital had to remain uneaten by me!

Through all the new facts I was absorbing there was one question which kept cropping up – why me? Why did I develop diabetes in the first place? There was no short and certain answer to this question then, and there still isn't. Apart from hereditary factors, experts cite three possible reasons for the development of diabetes; obesity, old age, severe shock. I was certainly not obese and nor was I old, which left shock. The diabetes was diagnosed a few days after the undeniably traumatic news that our family would be splitting up, so this has to be considered as a possible contributory factor. That said, I myself would hesitate to say categorically that this event caused my diabetes and I attach no blame whatsoever to my family. It is equally likely that a combination of causes led to my condition.

My father, who had been a professional footballer himself, was as depressed as I at the news of my illness. As he sat at my bedside when I was still in hospital after the diagnosis, I tried to cheer him up by saying: 'Don't worry Dad, I'll just have to be the first diabetic to play for England.' It was, in part, a flippant remark, a joke, but at the same time, it is every footballer's dream to represent his country and I had already played for the England Youth side on several occasions. It might have seemed increasingly unlikely, lying in hospital with a whole new life routine to learn, but I still had the goal of playing for England very firmly in my sights.

First things first, though, and that meant finding out how I would fare once back in training. The test came soon. When I came out of hospital Bristol Rovers had no game on the forthcoming Saturday, so the club were taking us for a mid-season break in Maguluf, Majorca. What I soon discovered was that training, or indeed playing, creates its own peculiar imbalances in the blood sugar level. A lot of sugar is used up with the amount of energy expended on strength and stamina exercises, so the level in the blood drops drastically.

I was initially advised to take sugar before training, so I was taking nine glucose tablets 20 minutes before each training session. When it came to matches, I took nine tablets beforehand and nine at half-time. Although it was very much a case of trial and error at this stage, I did come successfully through those training sessions in Majorca following this routine. I was up and playing football again, I wasn't thirsty the whole time and I wasn't lagging 50 yards behind the others. I felt fit, it was the best feeling in the world, because it meant that my career could continue.

One other thing which the trip to Majorca introduced me to, besides erratic blood sugar levels, was having to carry a syringe around with me wherever I went. As a very new diabetic, at that time I had not yet got a Government card which confirmed my condition and explained the syringe. I had visions of being stopped and having to explain what it was that I was carrying in a cassette box, which was obviously not a cassette, and that I was not carrying it because I was a drug addict! Fortunately, the baggage checking staff at Bristol airport must have read of my case in the local papers, because they knew who I was and there were no awkward questions. But it was another reminder, as if I needed one, that my newly acquired state would affect every aspect of my life.

It's also quite amusing when I look back, but in the hospital they came up with a novel suggestion about how I should cope with the demand on my sugar levels during a game ... the idea was for me to have a little pocket sewn into my football shorts and take lumps of sugar during the game at regular intervals! It was like schoolboy stuff. I said that in no way would that be practical. They came up with another plan ... let the referee carry the lumps of sugar for me!

But I kept taking the tablets, at least at first, and it worked wonders. I came through the critical initial two weeks of training and continued my football career.

CHAPTER TWO

HYPO ATTACKS ...
THE DAY I THOUGHT I DIED

In hospital, shortly after being diagnosed diabetic, they induced a 'hypo' attack, technically called hypoglacemic attack. I was warned that these attacks were the most dangerous aspect of everything I was going to have to face up to.

Quite simply, a 'hypo' attack is when the sugar level in the blood drops dangerously low and there is nothing to raise it to normal levels. This can occur, for example, if I were to take an insulin injection and then forget to eat the required amount of food 'exchanges', or didn't eat at all at the correct time. With the blood starved of sugar, the first place to be attacked is the brain. It can mean a drastic and often surprising change in character, as well as loss of physical control of your body.

I had an injection, but didn't eat for 20 minutes. The 'hypo' was, therefore, induced in the calm controlled atmosphere of the hospital. I felt weird sensations; sweaty, clammy palms, pins and needles in the tongue and lips, a numbness all over; I became very irritable. I was not the same person. All it takes is some sugar to return to normal and the recovery is so quick that it seems almost miraculous.

Of course, inducing an attack does not really prepare you for the time it happens in real life, but however it happens it is always a frightening experience.

I have suffered many 'hypo' attacks, but mostly only minor ones. For example, in the gym training, I'm running along quite normally one second, and then my legs buckle underneath me and I crumple in a heap, cutting my knees on the floor. I always hate to admit that something is wrong. That is part of the reaction in the way it affects the brain. It's crazy but I want to get up and get on with the training session – I pyschologically do not want to be helped. So I get up, take two steps and my legs go again.

I'll never forget the first time it happened after I had come to London to play for Spurs. Over I went in the gym, and Peter Shreeve volunteered: 'I'll get you some Lucozade'. It was the middle of winter, and it entailed going outside to get to the dressing rooms in the main stand. 'No', I insisted, 'I can manage myself'. Off I set to the dressing rooms desperately holding onto the bannister as I climbed down the stairs. I was shaking terribly. I stumbled in the snow outside. I crashed to the ground three times, ripping my knees to shreds, slapping them onto the concrete. The blood was pouring out. I found our physiotherapist Mike Varney and blurted out 'I'm low, I need Lucozade'. Once I had a drink I was fine – except for my knees!

The motto is that a diabetic must always carry sugar because a 'hypo' can strike at any time, any place. I'm obviously more vulnerable because of the amount of exercise I do, and the varying amount of strenuous work on any given day. What happened in the gym was far from funny, but there have been some amusing incidents.

When I first arrived in London I was living with my girlfriend Karen. We rented a house, and one day her family came for the weekend. We decided to cook them a meal and I took an injection 20 minutes before we were due to eat. Unfortunately the food took a little longer to cook than we had anticipated. When a 'hypo' attack builds up, the unsuspecting victim becomes irrational, sometimes extremely irrational – until the time they actually come round and then invariably they don't recall anything they got up to while under the influence. Now

I began to become stubborn and wanted to help Karen lay the table and, although I didn't know it at the time, I was becoming 'low'. I was carrying a massive jug of orange juice and, you've guessed it, I walked into the lounge, my legs gave way, I stumbled on a little further and then sent the orange juice, and glasses cascading all over the table and everyone sitting at it. Not satisfied with all that, I began shouting: 'Get away, I'll do it.' What happens is that I become annoyed with myself, and don't want anyone to help me. I went and sat upstairs for 10 to 15 minutes swearing at Karen, who was trying to give me some sugar in warm water. It must have been horrible for her and her family. I had made a complete fool of myself, but I didn't realise what I was doing, nor did I remember anything about it afterwards. Karen told me about it, though. All it took was a spoonful of sugar in some warm water and five or ten minutes later I was my normal self, right as rain. When Karen told me what I had done, I couldn't believe I was capable of it, it was a complete change in character ... very disconcerting.

My problem is that my sugar levels are continually going up and down at irregular times based on whenever I'm training or playing, travelling and eating different types of food with varying levels of sugar in them. When I'm eating regular meals with a stable pattern it is easier, but that is rarely possible in football.

I followed the initial routine of taking several glucose tablets before and during a match for about a year. But it was a job chewing the tablets, especially at half-time when my mouth was dry with the exertions of the first 45 minutes of high level, competitive football.

Beechams were good enough to work out that a can of Lucozade was about equivilent to the amount of glucose I was getting from the tablets. Drinking a can was a much more suitable way of raising my sugar level than munching tablets! I would drink a can of Lucozade before a game and three-quarters of a can at half-time.

Unfortunately there have been occasions when the attack has been serious. It has happened to me only a couple of times ...

but it has been two or three times too many for my liking.

One serious incident happened as I prepared for a midweek cup tie against Barnsley. Part of my routine, and most footballers' come to that, is to sleep in the afternoon prior to the game. I had now switched from my earlier schedule of two injections a day to four and also had a compact blood testing machine. This machine accurately reads the blood sugar level. I would have six to eight tests a day to work out the exact amount of insulin I would need.

We trained in the morning, I had lunch – a gammon steak – taking a blood test before the meal. I was surprised that the test showed quite high levels of sugar in my blood; afterall, I was about to eat, I hadn't just had my meal! It was pretty unusual. The reading on the machine was 18. A normal reading would show levels of between five and nine, so to compensate I injected twice the amount of insulin I would normally need for lunch. This sort of thing had happened before. I had worked out the right amounts before. Everything had been fine before.

I had my injection, then my lunch and went to bed at 1.30 pm. All I know from my side is waking up in hospital at 2.00 am the following morning. I've missed the cup tie. I haven't a clue what has happened. Everything else is a complete blank.

I have only managed to piece the rest of the story together accurately through information given to me by other people.

I've been told that I did not wake up, I did not turn up for the match at White Hart Lane and that at 6.30 pm, just an hour before kick-off, the management, staff and players in the team began to worry about me.

The team meeting went ahead as usual, but obviously without me. Everyone thought there must be a logical explanation. Was I perhaps held up in traffic? Generally I'm a punctual sort of person, I'm hardly ever late for training, let alone for an important cup tie. One or two people became frantic, knowing me well and knowing how unlike me it was to be so late. Some players are always late and they are continually being fined, but not usually me.

As it got closer and closer to kick-off time people started to wonder whether something really serious had happened. They knew that if there had been an accident I would have phoned in, or at least the police would have notified the club.

At 6.45 pm Ossie Ardiles, one of my closest friends at the time at the club, got really worried and thought it was about time to do something – to find out if I was OK. From the dressing rooms, with now just 35 minutes before he was due to trot out with the team in readiness for the cup tie, Ossie rang up one of Tottenham's former players, centre-half John Lacy, who lived two doors away from me.

'Can you go and see if Gary is alright? Have a look if there is a light on or see if his car is there', Ossie asked.

Big John Lacy was only too happy to help out and became concerned when he looked out of his window and couldn't see any lights on where I lived. He went round and looked in the garage, where my car was still parked. Fortunately, I had kept the back door open to let my Afghan hound walk in and out to the garden. John came in through the back door and started calling my name. He climbed the stairs to the bedroom, still calling my name. When he came through the door to my bedroom the sight that greeted him must have led him to think that I had been attacked. The entire room was turned upside down and I was lying naked on the floor, unconscious. There was blood all over the place.

There was blood all over my body, face, arms, legs – all over the bed, behind the bed, on the walls, on the curtains. I had cut myself all over. What had happened was that I had tried to give myself a blood test, and was so 'low' that I was unable to do so, and kept cutting myself.

I was out cold. John could get no sense out of me. But he noticed that I once opened my eyes, although all there was was a glazed look. It must have been frightening for him, and he couldn't be sure what had happened. He snapped to his senses and remembered that amongst our neighbours there was a couple, both of whom were doctors. He rushed over and the wife was there, the husband out on his calls.

27

Knowing that I was a diabetic she tried to give me some sugar, but I was in no condition to take it. Her husband soon arrived on the scene. They decided to give me a glucose injection straight into my veins ... I still didn't come round. That was the point where they both began to worry. It is normal to come round after the sugar level in the blood is restored. An ambulance was called and I was rushed to Queen Elizabeth Hospital in Welwyn Garden City. It was felt that once they got me to hospital I would be alright – although that was what they had thought once I was found and given the sugar!

When I finally woke up there I was with *two* drips in my arm feeding me glucose intravenously. Just imagine how I felt. I didn't know where I was or how I'd got there. I saw two nurses and asked them: 'What's happened?' They started to explain that I had fallen into a deep diabetic coma.

The next thing I thought about was the game. I was supposed to have been playing against Barnsley. 'How did Spurs get on?' I asked the nurses. They didn't have a clue. Perhaps I should have been more concerned with the fact that I was lucky to be alive, rather than that I had missed the game. But my main reaction was sheer shock. What had happened? I just couldn't work out what had gone wrong. I had always gone for an afternoon nap before a game, and if ever I was going 'low' that would normally be a good wake up call!

Remarkably, the next morning when John Lacy walked into the hospital to visit I was fine, absolutely nothing wrong! I'd even got up out of bed. Of course I looked terrible, unshaven, no clothes, but I was ready to go. John had kindly brought me one of my track suits and drove me straight round to White Hart Lane.

I began training! I was running around the track by myself as good as new. The manager, David Pleat, asked me how I felt and I said: 'Absolutely fine'. He looked unsure, was no doubt still concerned, and said he would take advice before considering whether to play me that weekend.

As it turned out I got the all-clear, travelled up to Liverpool on the Friday with the team and played at Anfield – I was delighted that I had a good game. Thursday I was in hospital, Saturday I was playing. That shows you just how quickly it can all change round.

It always crosses my mind as to whether I let the team down because of missing the Barnsley cup tie. I have often considered it, but as it was a complete accident, almost a fluke, and as it was a one-off, I can't say I feel guilty. I couldn't do anything about it at the time. It was out of my control.

My priority afterwards was to investigate what happened, and why it happened, in order to ensure there was no repeat performance.

Once again, this incident was kept out of the papers – at least, the full impact and implications of it. But the fact that I missed a match, and a Littlewoods Cup tie at that, made it difficult to avoid facing the media and offering an explanation.

At the time the club were naturally very concerned about the media coverage. They were worried about any exaggeration, distortion, or sensationalisation. The official line was that I had missed the game because I changed the type of insulin I take. It was put out as not being very serious. I was simply feeling ill, to ill to play.

The truth was that it had been very serious, and might easily have been fatal. What happened was that my blood testing machine had gone wrong. In addition to the test done by the machine, there's a second, 'manual' one which can be done to back up the machine reading. This is done by taking a sample of blood on the end of a spatula and reading it against a coloured chart. Normally it is only necessary to do the machine test. On this occasion the machine gave me a reading of 19 when the normal level is between five and nine.

Because that was a disturbing reading I did the test with the coloured chart, which gave a reading of nine or ten. As this was still higher than normal I injected myself with twice the usual amount of insulin straightaway.

The blood testing machine had given me the wrong reading. I had dropped the machine onto the concrete, out of my bag, a few days earlier and this must have caused it to go wrong. I thought nothing of it at the time.

I changed the machine straightaway – in fact within a day I had a new portable machine, which is now regularly serviced.

In reality, I have had precious few very serious attacks, and for that I can only be thankful.

On a much lighter note, however, there are often embarrassing moments for me.

For example, I once had a 'hypo' attack in the middle of signing autographs for a large group of schoolchildren outside our former training headquarters at Cheshunt. Suddenly, I just stopped signing, and I didn't really know where I was. Fortunately, Chris Waddle came out of the changing rooms just at the right time to come to my rescue. Once he spotted what was happening he immediately ordered the people back. He put my arm around his neck and dragged me back to the dressing rooms. He gave me some sugar and after 10 minutes I was asking him 'What's wrong, what's been happening?' Chris explained it all, and that is really the worst thing about these incidents – being told what I did when I can't remember, and when I'd rather not have done it anyway!

CHAPTER THREE

GUINEA PIG

Although I'm evidently not the only person around suffering with diabetes, I remain something of a test case, a guinea pig even, as far as the specialists are concerned. Where my case differs from many is in the daily rigours I put my body through, training and performing as a professional sportsman. Experts are keen to find out just what kind of effect such a routine has, when the body involved is also dealing with diabetes. One such expert is Edwin Gale and, though he doesn't normally take on private patients, he has made an exception in my case in order to study my specific experiences. I think it probably intrigues me as much as him!

Most diabetics know of the problems their condition can bring. The areas which most often deteriorate are the eyes and nerve endings – which can lead to amputation becoming necessary in some instances. However, there seems little point, to me, in being afraid of the future. I made my decision to carry on playing football at the top level. I shall never regret that decision.

Among the multitude of letters I receive is a large proportion from active sportsmen and women. They are, quite naturally, concerned about the possibilities of one of the complications of diabetes setting in early because of their devotion to sport and participation in it. Of course it can happen, but you can't say it definitely will. Nothing will alter my basic belief that it is possible to lead a normal life despite being a diabetic.

The truth is that the specialists are so far, touch wood, impressed with the way my body has coped with the demands of professional football for so long.

That said, the operation I underwent on my left foot after the 1987 FA Cup Final defeat by Coventry was undeniably linked to diabetes. There was a blood supply problem to my left foot. As I've already said, diabetes affects the nerve endings in the body and also the blood vessels. The foot is supplied by one main channel leading to the heel and one down the front of the foot. The channel down the back of the foot became blocked, leaving the whole supply via the front channel.

When I exercise, the blood vessels enlarge and there are muscles which enable that function to occur. I needed an operation to prevent those muscles contracting, so the blood vessels would remain as large as they possibly can be to allow the free flow of the blood to and from the leg and foot.

The operation, which actually took place on an area of the spine, was a total success. So much so that my left foot remains bone dry. I could wear the warmest sock and it would still be perfectly dry. It just never sweats.

I should add that this type of complaint is probably more common in older diabetics than one of my age at the time of the surgery.

An example of how much my diabetes has become accepted in the football world stems from this operation. At the time Liverpool were desperately keen to sign me. My contract was at an end at Spurs, but I was deeply involved in negotiations to stay at White Hart Lane. Yet Kenny Dalglish made contact and was equally determined to sign me. He was made fully aware that the operation was related to my peculiar situation but it made no difference to him. He said: 'We know what you are capable of, we've seen you play, and we know your appearance record. We're not worried.'

In fact I was wanted by Lyon in France (who were also trying to sign Steve Archibald at the time), Arsenal, Manchester United, Everton and Derby (who were also signing Peter

Elmlea school football team (front row, second from right)

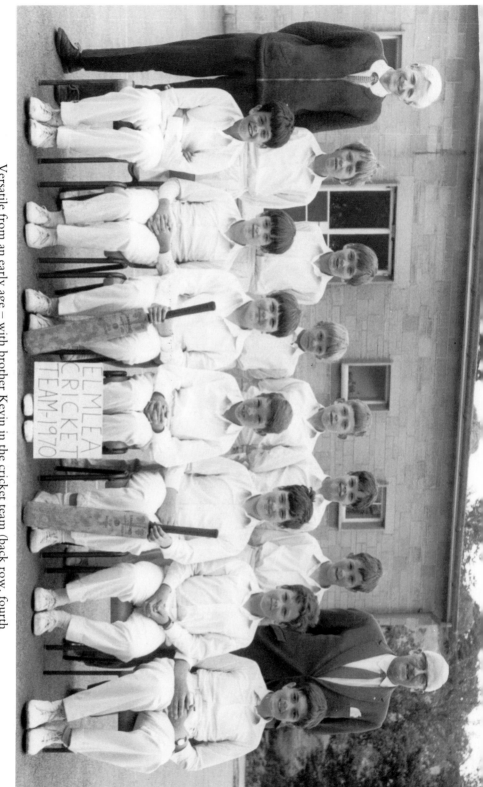

Versatile from an early age – with brother Kevin in the cricket team (back row, fourth and third from left respectively)

Signing up as an apprentice for Bristol Rovers, summer 1977, flanked by Don Megson (left) and my father

In action for Rovers

Celebrating after scoring the first goal in the England U-21 victory over Denmark 4-1,
September 1982
Photo: Bob Thomas

Newly signed for Spurs, with Keith Burkinshaw (left) and Peter Shreeve
Photo: Daily Star

Taking on Johann Cruyff
Photo: Bob Thomas

Photo: Bob Thomas

Training with England in Budapest, October 1983
Photo: Bob Thomas

A near miss in the subsequent match against Hungary
Photos: Frank Tewkesbury for The London Evening Standard

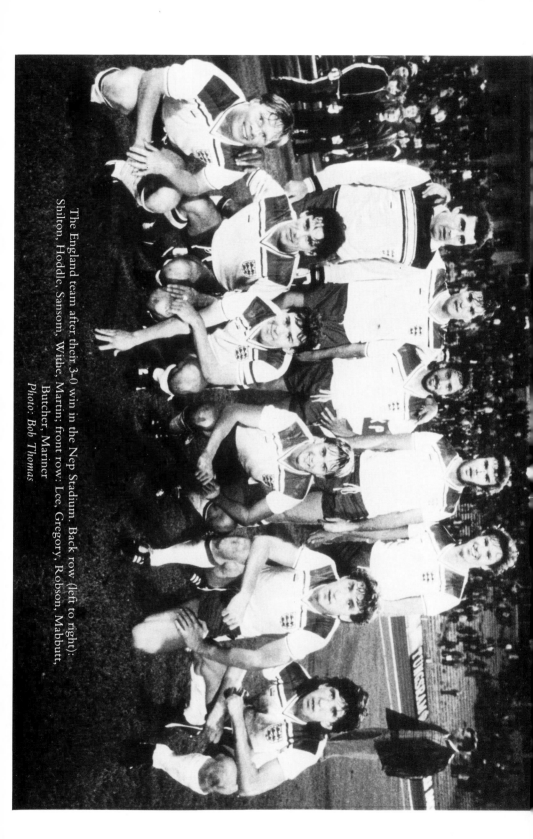

The England team after their 3-0 win in the Nep Stadium. Back row (left to right): Shilton, Hoddle, Sansom, Withe, Martin; front row: Lee, Gregory, Robson, Mabbutt, Butcher, Mariner

Photo: Bob Thomas

Getting to grips with McAvennie of West Ham, December 1986
Photo: Action Images

Getting the better of McAvennie with a spectacular challenge
Photo: *Action Images*

In a tangle with John Fashanu of Wimbledon
Photo: Times Newspapers Ltd

Tottenham training session with Richard Gough (centre) and Mitchell Thomas
Photo: Action Images

Shilton).

As it turned out, I decided to re-sign for Spurs, and I'm glad that I did. Spurs are a fabulous club and I feel proud and privileged to be their skipper.

Naturally, there are incidents, both on and off the football pitch, which would not have occurred, were it not for my diabetes. For instance, after one match against Nottingham Forest several of the Spurs players went on to a Hot Chocolate concert. Afterwards we were all invited back by the group to the Cromwellian Club in Knightsbridge for a private party. I hadn't had time to eat before I went out so I was hungry and made for the large buffet provided. Before tucking in, though, I needed an injection. I always carry all that I need in my travelling cassette case. I went downstairs to the toilet. It was just a tiny bit tricky – there were no private cubicles for me to go into.

So, there I was, syringe in hand, phial in my lap, withdrawing the insulin in readiness for the injection, when in walked three men.

It's not hard to guess at their thoughts; a pop concert party, someone in the gents about to inject himself ... obvious isn't it? I attempted to explain that it wasn't as obvious as they thought, but they didn't seem to want to listen, and they didn't believe me anyway. They probably thought I was trying to cover up with a lame excuse. They called me a disgrace and said: 'You shouldn't be doing this sort of thing.'

I quickly injected myself and left. I told the other players about it and they all had a good laugh. Then it was my round so off I went to the bar. Just my luck. At the bar were the three who had burst in on me in the toilets. 'So diabetics do drink then?' they said, with just a hint of sarcasm!

That sort of thing happens quite a bit. I'd be sitting on the toilet in a hotel or restaurant. I'm on the point of drawing the insulin into the syringe and in bursts somebody pushing the door open – and of course they get the wrong idea immediately.

There's also no doubt that one popular misconception of a diabetic is that he or she is handicapped.

Football supporters are notoriously cruel in their baiting of players and they never miss an opportunity. When I take a throw in and I'm close to the terraces, within earshot of the supporters, I can hear the jibes of the opposition fans. I've been called a cripple and a junkie.

In one game at Goodison Park in 1987 I was taking a throw in, just about to deliver the throw, when a whole bag of Barker and Dobson sweets hit me on the back of the head. 'Eat those you spastic,' bawled an Everton fan. As any diabetic will tell you, you're not allowed to eat sweets. In fact that's pretty common knowledge. So I found the incident quite amusing at the time. Junkie is a jibe I hear quite a lot.

The trouble with diabetes – and the factor which leads to these kinds of incident – is ignorance. To be honest I knew precious little on the subject before it all happened to me, so I'm not really complaining, merely stating a point of view. But the more people know, the better their appreciation of a diabetic's problems.

All footballers take a certain amount of stick on the pitch and if I have to cope with my share of it – well, I see it as part of the job really.

When I first moved to Tottenham I became big news mainly *because* of my diabetes.

Suddenly everyone knew about it. The British Diabetic Association use me to try and provide a truer understanding of diabetes. This began when I contacted them for guidance when I was first diagnosed. Then, when I signed for Spurs, they contacted me.

They have branches in every town in the country. I have been invited to numerous meetings to give lectures and I try to attend whenever possible.

I have been to quite a few diabetic clinics and hospital centres where question and answer sessions are held. At such events I explain how diabetes has affected me, the problems I've had to face, and often give as an example my daily routine:

8.00 am … Wake up early in preparation for training.

8.10 am … Have the first of four daily injections. It would be 14 units of Actrapid insulin.

8.30 am ... Breakfast of cereal, either Rice Krispies or corn flakes (no Sugar Puffs!). Within half an hour of the first injection I must have 40g of carbohydrate. To make it a bit easier for diabetics to know what they are eating in terms of carbohydrate, each type of food is given a rating and the term used for this is an 'exchange'. An 'exchange' is 10g worth of carbohydrate. So for breakfast I need four 'exchanges' – the cereal being worth three and a Rich Tea biscuit, or thin slice of toast, one.

10.20 am ... Arrive at the training ground. Drink one can of Lucozade.

10.30 am ... Start training. There is always the danger of a 'hypo' occurring because it is impossible to know whether we will have a long or short training session. If I feel I'm going 'low' I will send one of the apprentices or young lads to the dressing room for another can of Lucozade.

12.30 pm ... Normal time to finish training.

1.00 pm ... Arrive home. Time for the second injection of the day. (This time eight units of Actrapid insulin).

1.30 pm ... Lunch must now consist of four 'exchanges'; a snack of either a toasted cheese sandwich or big jacket potato.

2.00 pm ... I'm involved in a property company and I might spend some time on that business, or I could be involved in opening a shop or supermarket, or coaching.

3.30 pm ... I must have two 'exchanges', normally they would be biscuits.

6.30 pm ... Third injection. (14 units of Actrapid).

7.00 pm ... Main meal of the day consisting of eight 'exchanges'. I would either eat out or cook myself a meal of soup (represents between two and three 'exchanges'), chicken, fillet steak or

35

fish (which, as protein, are worth nothing on the 'exchanges' scale) with chips or jacket potato (equals three 'exchanges') and peas (one 'exchange'). The last course is one slice of vanilla ice cream (one 'exchange') or a pear (one 'exchange'). If I'm out with friends or it's a special occasion I would drink dry wine or champagne. Champagne is the best alcoholic drink for a diabetic because it contains little sugar – what's more, I enjoy it! But as a rule a diabetic should not drink alcohol to excess as it lowers the blood sugar level and then there is always the danger of a 'hypo'.

Also there is another real danger; if a diabetic is in trouble and he is found smelling of drink, he could end up in a cell mistaken for a drunk, only to be found the next morning ... dead. This has been known to happen.

11.00 pm ... Last of the daily injections, being 32 units of Insulatard, followed by four 'exchanges' – most likely a sandwich or biscuits.

CHAPTER FOUR

RISK

When any footballer is transferred between clubs one of the pre-requisites of the deal is a medical. When I moved from Bristol Rovers to Tottenham the medical had special significance for obvious reasons.

I was sent to a specialist as Spurs, quite rightly, needed to have expert advice on my condition. Physiotherapist Mike Varney took me to a clinic in Enfield. I was not unduly concerned. I had proved in the previous two years at Bristol Rovers that I could play on despite diabetes.

The club were informed that it was alright for me to pursue a football career, even at the highest level, with all the stress and strain that would impose on my body, for the next 10 years at least, without any ill-effect within that time. No-one could tell the club, nor could they reassure me, that there would not be any serious knock-on effects in the long term. The risks are known: I was more than ready to take them. I was determined to make sure that my diabetes would live with me, rather than allow it to rule my life.

I noticed an advertising campaign at the beginning of 1989 ... 'X per cent of diabetics end up with blindness, kidney failure or amputations.' The object was to make people stop and think, in order to raise money to try to find a cure. The British Diabetic Association would normally consider me for such campaigns, but there was no point in this case. A huge picture of me in

England kit, or running out with the Spurs team, wouldn't persuade too many people to part with their money. Their attitude would probably be: 'Well, he looks alright to me!' Clearly, I was not the right man for that particular campaign as my philosophy is that I can lead a relatively normal life. I would add, though, that considerable research into diabetes is still very much needed – along with the funds to finance it.

However, there can be no doubt that clubs in general were sceptical in the extreme about taking me on when my contract with Bristol Rovers expired in the summer of 1982. Rovers had turned down a couple of offers two or three months before my contract ran out, one of them from Watford. But the club were struggling financially and wanted to sell me for a reasonable price.

Bobby Gould was my manager at Rovers, and at this time Luton were on the way up to the First Division. Their manager, David Pleat, was very interested in signing me to play at left-back, even though my position with Rovers at the time was centre-half.

In fact, so keen was Bobby Gould to sell me to Luton that he even agreed to David Pleat's request to play me at left-back in Rovers' final few games of the season, so he could scrutinise my performances in that position!

After this extraordinary 'trial' for Luton, David Pleat was still not totally convinced. Rovers Reserves were playing at Luton and he asked Bobby Gould to play me in that game … again at left-back. When Bobby rang me to tell me about it I could tell he wasn't too sure himself about this little exercise. Well, I agreed, even though I thought it was all very odd.

I played, and the following day Bobby rang me again. He said: 'Luton want to sign you. They have finally made up their minds, they want you to see them tomorrow and play for them on Saturday.'

Luton were in such good form, and comfortably ahead in the promotion race, I knew that if I signed with them I would be playing first division football the following season. I was therefore naturally very keen to sign. Bobby Gould, the Rovers secretary Gordon Bennett, and my father accompanied me to Luton for talks. The idea was to get the whole deal settled as quickly as possible.

We met David Pleat, Luton's secretary and their chief executive in the Post House Hotel on the motorway half way between the two clubs. I first spoke to David Pleat with my father present.

I found David Pleat to be very impressive and persuasive. He told me how much he wanted me to play for his club and where he wanted me to play. I told him I was anxious for first division football and equally keen to sign, and play, for him. It was a coincidence, but my family comes from Aylesbury and that made the prospect of signing for Luton even more attractive. I said to David Pleat: 'It all sounds great to me'.

Then the conversation got round to finances.

Luton offered me a salary of £50 a week *less* than Bristol Rovers were paying me in the third division, and here I was about to move up into the First. I couldn't believe it. My dad told me that if I agreed to sign this contract I wouldn't be able to keep up the mortgage payments on my house! It was ridiculous. I was going to hit the big time and earn less money. I was asked, if I wanted, to think over the offer. Well, I didn't need much thinking time before I went back to David Pleat with my answer ... 'no'. He got my decision on the spot. On the basis of that offer I cannot believe anyone would have signed.

On the journey home Bobby Gould was far from happy with my decision to reject Luton. It was obvious that the club needed money and that he wanted me to sign for them. But I wouldn't, on a point of principle. For the next couple of days there were frequent conversations and renegotiations and increased offers.

Luton came within £15-20 difference, but were still short and there was no way I could accept. If they had offered me the same amount of money I would have signed, as I was only too ready to join them. But I'd have been moving to a more expensive area for less money and it just didn't seem right.

Suddenly it all came to a head. Bobby Gould called me into

his office. He was on the phone. He told me: 'I've got David Pleat on the end of this line.' He went on: 'This is your last opportunity to sign for Luton. Here are two good young managers trying to do you a favour. You may regret it if you don't grasp this golden chance.'

But the offer remained on the same terms as before, still less than I was earning at Bristol Rovers.

'No', I wouldn't do it.

'You heard that, David', said Bobby Gould, 'I'm very sorry but the answer is no'.

I then got a lecture from Bobby Gould who told me I had messed around two good managers who were trying to do the best for me. 'Go on then, get out training', was his last comment on the subject.

At the end of that season my contract came to an end, and after the last game, when I was officially able to decide my own future, I wrote to every first division club. I set out how many league games I'd played without any ill effects, that I had won 11 England Youth caps and played so many times for the England Under-21 team. 'Please get in touch', I wrote.

I received just two replies. One came from Birmingham City manager Ron Saunders. He was very encouraging and said he wanted to speak to me as soon as he could. The other reply came from Aston Villa: 'I'm sorry we are unable to offer you a trial'. So much for Villa. But at least they had the courtesy to reply.

I travelled up to St. Andrews and was very impressed with the set up at Birmingham. I was told that they intended to buy a few more players and wanted to go places. They wanted me to play on the right-hand side of midfield. However, they couldn't sign me straightaway. There was a snag. They were awaiting money from their sale of Jo Gallagher, which was an independent tribunal decision. They needed that money before they could buy me.

I was quite happy to sign for Birmingham after talking with them, but they stressed that there would have to be a delay of about six weeks. There were still three of these six weeks to go when I had made arrangements for a holiday in Corfu. Three days before I was due to depart I received a call from Bobby Gould. 'Tottenham Hotspur want you', he said. I could hardly believe it … even though, I must confess, I did have an inkling they might come in.

My girlfriend Karen was sharing digs with the assistant secretary of Bristol Rovers. This room-mate had actually received a call from Bill Nicholson and she had told Karen about it. We had only been going out for a few weeks and Karen wasn't that much into football. So she didn't know what a bombshell she was dropping when she said: 'Oh, by the way Gary, don't say anything to my friend, but she had a call from Tottenham Hotspur and passed it on to Bobby Gould. They are interested in signing you.' I thought I must have been dreaming and was sure she must have got it wrong.

However, the next day Bobby Gould rang to tell me the same thing! Somehow I managed to sound totally surprised all over again – the news was stunning enough for me not to have to act too hard.

After such a struggle to convince a first division club that I was good enough, and that diabetes would not affect me at the highest level, and with only one showing any interest, right out of the blue one of the top clubs in the country was after me. I was stunned. But, quite naturally, pleasantly surprised, and very pleased.

Bobby Gould explained that Bill Nicholson wanted to speak to me because Spurs manager Keith Burkinshaw and his assistant Peter Shreeve were away at the World Cup in Spain. 'I've explained the Birmingham City situation', said Bobby Gould, 'but Bill Nicholson has asked me to ask you not to sign for them until you've given Spurs the chance to speak to you first.'

I was committed to my holiday, in fact the day after Bobby Gould rang me I was off. But I went away deliriously happy. Spurs had just won the FA Cup for the second successive season; they were recognised as one of the best clubs in world football; and all of a sudden they were interested in me. It was a great holiday!

When I returned from my holiday Tottenham had already begun their pre-season training, four days ahead of Bristol Rovers. I travelled to White Hart Lane to meet Bill Nicholson and was taken to the Cheshunt training ground to be introduced to Keith Burkinshaw and Peter Shreeve. The manager took me for a stroll and said: 'Look, I want to sign you – what position do you play?' I think he meant to inquire about what my best position was! I told him that I preferred midfield, but that I could play in all the defensive positions.

Keith Burkinshaw told me straight that I should be under no illusion, I was considered to be an asset to the club but he was not buying me to walk straight into the first team. Spurs were a team full of stars such as Ray Clemence, Steve Perryman, Glenn Hoddle, Ricky Villa, Ossie Ardiles, Garth Crooks, and Steve Archibald. It was like a Who's Who of footballers. For somebody coming out of third division Bristol Rovers it was like a dream – sounds corny but it's true. I was like a starry eyed kid.

I only knew Terry Gibson because I had played with him in the England Youth team and also Peter Southey (who has since tragically died), but at least it was reassuring to see a couple of familiar, friendly faces. To be honest, the contract offered by Spurs only just beat the money I was on at Bristol Rovers, but at least it was a rise and I was on my way to a top first division club. I had no hesitation in agreeing to the move.

I rang Ron Saunders at Birmingham City to inform him that I had decided to sign for Spurs. I thought it would be a difficult conversation, but I was pleasantly surprised by his reaction. He understood perfectly. 'Fine, that's your decision', he said. He wished me all the best and good luck in my career.

A small footnote to my brief encounter with Birmingham City, is that while I was in hospital first suffering with diabetes, Jasper Carrott sent me a card saying: 'See you in Division One – Good Luck' He was a director of Birmingham at the time ... and then I nearly signed for his club!

As for Spurs, I had no doubts in mind. I was going to a club that was so big I fully expected to play in the reserves for the first two years and wait patiently for my first taste of first team football. I was more than prepared to wait and learn from all the great players at the club.

I have often wondered why Spurs decided to come in for me, and I've heard a variety of stories. I have been told that Peter Anderson, then manager of Millwall, was very keen on me but when he heard the price was £125,000 he dropped out. Because he often took advice from Bill Nicholson in his early managerial days and kept in close contact with him, he rang Bill to tell him: 'If you're looking for a good squad player why don't you go for Gary Mabbutt?'

I'm also told that Bill said that I would probably cost too much. When Peter Anderson told him the price he had been quoted Bill became very interested. Of course £125,000 was a lot of money for Millwall at that time, but not a big fee for a club as wealthy as Spurs.

CHAPTER FIVE

ENGLAND

'I thought he was bionic. It was staggering the amount of ground he covered'.

So said Bobby Robson of my performance for the England Under-21 team against Denmark. I had played at left-back and had scored twice in our 4-1 win, but nevertheless, being labelled 'bionic' is something to live up to!

It was September 1982 and Robson was in charge of the country's football team for the first time, with the senior team due to play an important European Championship qualifier in Denmark. I collected quite a few complimentary mentions in the press following my two goals for the Under-21s, and that obviously pleased me enormously. The only thing about reading your own press is that, for all the good things that are written about you from time to time, there are certainly as many bad. Still, at that stage I was being tipped to make my full international debut in the match against West Germany scheduled for October 13.

Steve Curry in the *Daily Express*: 'Mabbutt seems to have grown in confidence since his move to Spurs in the summer. He scored both his goals from the left-back position, as he has done twice for Spurs, proving he is an all-purpose performer … described as 'bionic' by Robson, (he) looks ready now for the challenge of senior international soccer'.

As predicted, I did make my full England debut against West

Germany and with it part of the prophecy made to my dad in my hospital bed when I was first diagnosed diabetic had come true.

I was first called up as an England player for the youth team when I was a humble third division performer with Bristol Rovers. I was star struck when I turned up for the three-day training sessions each month with England Youth coach John Cartwright, with players around like Tommy Caton, Steve MacKenzie and Clive Allen.

The first match I was involved with was against Italy in Rome. I was substitute and shared a room with Clive Allen – later, of course, to be a Tottenham team-mate. Colin Pates, Andy Peak, and Paul Allen, another future team-mate, were also in that line-up.

The next match was a Mini-World Cup qualifying game against Denmark at Coventry. We won 4-0 with Mark Hateley getting all four. The Tottenham connections were springing up all the time, as Danny Thomas was in that side, along with Terry Gibson and Tommy English.

It was definitely a thrill for a player from the lower divisions to play alongside these first division lads. At that time Steve MacKenzie was becoming a sensation as he became the costliest 17-year-old, when big-spending Malcolm Allison paid his old club Crystal Palace £250,000 to take the midfield player to Manchester City.

Youth coach John Cartwright was a man I much admired and I was sure he would progress to a top club in this country, or even to international level. Instead he went to Saudi Arabia after Crystal Palace, and returned as coach at Arsenal. At the time I was training under him with the English Youth team, he was experimenting with the 'libero' system, following the example of the Continentals, particularly the Italians. I had been playing midfield, but he tried me out as sweeper and also at centre-half – from an early stage I was singled out as a versatile player. John was a brave coach and caused an uproar when he dropped Manchester City star Tommy Caton to play me at the back. Immediately the Press were on his back: 'How

46

can you leave out Caton?' However, the team won 4-0.

My first time as captain of the England Youth team was in a European Championship qualifying game against Denmark. We won 2-0 and the squad included another future Tottenham link, Paul Walsh. It is a great honour to captain your country at any level and I still have the shirt and captain's armband from that match.

Next came a 10-day tournament in Pula, Yugoslavia at the start of the season. There I scored my first goal for my country. I'll never forget it. A chipped through ball and a left foot, first time drive into the left hand corner. Once again, it felt very special to be on my first England trip abroad, part of the England set-up.

The next time I travelled abroad with England, it was as a diabetic. Fortunately, because I was back playing just three weeks after being diagnosed, it did not affect my progress with England. Professor O'Gorman was the England doctor at the time and there can be no doubt that his opinion was sought before I was picked again.

He was certainly consulted about how best to look after me when the England Youth team went to East Germany at the end of the season for a vital European Championship qualifying match.

There was a special consignment of dozens of packets of McVities digestive biscuits, intravenous glucose, and dextrosol tablets because there was no telling the sort of food I would find in Leipzig.

As it turned out I desperately needed those digestive biscuits! The meals were all protein – meat or fish – with a soup starter. There were hardly any carbohydrates such as potatoes or bread. As we were at Lilleshall for a week's training and in Leipzig for nine days, I was virtually living on biscuits. Every meal in East Germany I would eat with the team, bringing my biscuits with me to finish off!

To add to the difficulty of the trip, there was nothing to occupy our minds. Fortunately John Cartwright broke the monotony by organising snooker competitions and games at the hotel. The hotel did not have large enough rooms for us to share, so we were billetted in single rooms. The rooms had no baths, just a tiny shower in the corner. 'Walkman' personal stereos hadn't come in yet, but Tommy Caton brought with him a massive music centre, and we spent a lot of our time sitting in the hotel corridors listening to music. It worked. We won the tournament. We got the song sheets out and sang all the way back from the stadium to the hotel. However difficult the trip had been, this made it all worthwhile.

We played Poland in the final of the European Championships, beating them 2-1. All in all I played 11 times for the England Youth team before progressing to the Under-21s at the age of 19, when still at Bristol Rovers.

Oddly, I owe my early Under-21 call to the snow! The match was taking place at the County Ground Swindon against Rumania. There was so much snow that some players were unable to report for the game, so because I was close at hand in Bristol, I was summoned to the team hotel on the Sunday night. Most players knew each other, either from previous squads or from first division matches. When they saw me they must have said: 'Who is this lad from Bristol Rovers?' I had no trouble recognising them. The squad was packed with first division stars; Remi Moses, Gary Owen, Garry Thompson and Justin Fashanu. I was on the bench with Clive Allen and Vince Hilaire.

Even though I didn't kick a ball, as I didn't leave the substitutes bench, the manager of the senior England team, Ron Greenwood, thanked me for turning up. That was compensation enough for not getting a game – really just involvement in the squad at that stage was ample reward.

The following year I made my debut at Under-21 level in Poland. It was at the time of all the political trouble with Solidarity and Lech Walesa. When our plane landed we were greeted by armed guards. There was a 9 pm curfew and we were not allowed out of our hotel. All we saw of Warsaw was the coach journey from airport to hotel, from hotel to the stadium for training, and then to the match. Although there was a big crowd it was all army personnel. I played left-back.

48

We won 1-0. Apart from football, the trip was certainly an eye-opener for someone who'd never before been to that part of the world.

We might have gone out of the European Championships in the second leg of that tie with Poland at West Ham, but didn't, thanks to Ian Hesford saving a penalty.

The semi-final was against the Scots at Hampden Park. I played on the left side of midfield. We won 1-0. It was great to be able to go back to Bristol and tell everyone at the club about the day we beat the Scots at Hampden! I was substitute for the return game with Scotland when we went through to the final on aggregate. That was my last game for the Under-21s before joining Tottenham.

I was signed by Spurs as a squad player – though for a squad player I had a pretty eventful first few weeks! I began the season at Wembley in the Charity Shield against Liverpool and after a month I had scored twice in front of the new England manager Bobby Robson for the Under-21s in Denmark. The following Saturday I scored twice in Spurs' 4-1 win over Nottingham Forest. The late Bernard Joy wrote in the *Sunday Express*: 'Versatile Gary Mabbutt, labelled "bionic" by England manager Bobby Robson for his two goals against Denmark's Under-21s on Tuesday, enhanced his prestige with two more in another dynamic performance. "He's a fair player" said manager Keith Burkinshaw with typical Northern understatement.'

I had already played in five positions for Spurs since my transfer from Rovers. I got my fifth goal in a week in Spurs' 4-0 win over Coleraine, and the prediction that I would make my England debut against World Cup Finalists West Germany was fulfilled.

Three months with Spurs and I was an England player. When Robson named the squad I was one of four newcomers in the 22, together with John Barnes, Luther Blissett and Mark Chamberlain. I heard the news I had always longed for in a dentist's chair! I was having a filling done by the club dentist with Radio 2 on in the background. It was still a shock, even though the press had been building it up that I would be in the squad. You can never be sure until you are actually, officially named – it was a real case of the agony and the ecstasy in that dentist's chair.

The following week I joined up with the squad at the West Lodge Park Hotel. I just couldn't believe I was there. The manager normally picks his England team on the Tuesday, the day before the international. Bobby Robson took the unusual step of telling me on the Monday after training that not only was I in the squad, but I would be in the team. He said that he was considering playing me in a central defensive position, but because Bryan Robson had pulled out with an injury I would definitely be playing in midfield.

However, in a training session on the morning of the game John Barnes collided with Viv Anderson, who dislocated his knee. England team doctor Vernon Edwards manipulated Viv's knee back into place and then he was taken off to hospital. The manager called me over and said: 'Can you play at right-back?' Well, I had played in so many positions, right-back was not going to be a problem. Michael Hart in the *Evening Standard* quoted the England manager: 'That's his third position in 24 hours. I've no worries about him at all. He's an extremely versatile lad'.

Southampton's left-sided forward David Armstrong was the other new cap besides me. The team was: Peter Shilton (Southampton), Gary Mabbutt (Spurs), Phil Thompson (Liverpool), Terry Butcher (Ipswich), Kenny Sansom (Arsenal), David Armstrong (Southampton), Ray Wilkins (Man Utd), Ricky Hill (Luton), Cyrille Regis (WBA), Paul Mariner (Ipswich), Alan Devonshire (West Ham); Subs, Gary Bailey (Man Utd), Alvin Martin (West Ham), Graham Rix (Arsenal), Tony Woodcock (Arsenal), Luther Blissett (Watford).

The Germans were a formidable team: Schumacher, Kaltz, Strack, Karl-Heinz Forster, B. Forster, Dremmier, Briegel, Meier, Allofs, Matthaus, Rummenigge.

All the Mabbutts turned out. The thrill of pulling on that white shirt of England, and at Wembley too, was a dream come true. Corny. But, I have to admit, it's true. As I stood in the tunnel waiting to come out it finally sank in that I was realising my ambition to play for my country. I walked out with the team and Wembley was packed – virtually all English supporters. The noise was deafening. Lining up for the National anthem, I spotted my family and gave them a wave. I was proud, excited, and determined to enjoy it. And I did enjoy it, even though we played one of the best teams in the world and Karl-Heinz Rummenigge put the Germans two up, which was destined to bring to an end England's run of 13 matches without defeat.

The game might have turned had my 35th minute shot not hit a post. It seems Spurs players have a knack of scoring on their England debuts at Wembley. Glenn Hoddle did it against Bulgaria, and Paul Gascoigne managed it as a late substitute against Albania. I was unlucky. The ball came to me outside the box from a corner and I drove it left footed on the half volley. I thought it was in. The shot beat Harald Schumacher ... hit the foot of the post ... and came out. I also had a header cleared off the line. I was not destined to score. Our one goal came from substitute Tony Woodcock.

David Miller wrote in the *Express*: 'Why did almost everyone enjoy England's performance in defeat? For the good reason that we saw, in Devonshire, Ricky Hill, Cyrille Regis, and Gary Mabbutt, some of the running at defenders and dribbling which is what the public yearns for.'

Most of my 13 caps were won in my first season at Spurs. In November, I played in the European Championship qualifying game against Greece in Salonika. There was a pretty hostile reception from the Greek crowd, and we needed an armed escort to go training. There would be a police van in front of the team coach and one behind full of armed guards. Their fans taunted us and even besieged our hotel, shouting abuse at us if we appeared. We won 3-0 and the *Sunday Express* reporter wrote: 'Mabbutt's performance in Greece may be a harbinger of England's future under Robson. They have come together at the same time, Robson as manager and Mabbutt as player. Mabbutt's leap to the top with Spurs has been astonishing. Last season he was in the third division with Bristol Rovers and was bought in the summer for a modest £125,000 with no greater promise than a place in Spurs' first team squad. The deal may qualify as the best piece of business of the season.'

In December I played in midfield against Luxembourg at Wembley where we recorded a fantastic 9-0 victory. In October 1983 I played against Hungary in Budapest in yet another role, as a man-to-man marker against their talented midfield star Tibor Nyalisi. We won 3-0 to keep hopes of a European Championship qualification flickering.

Steve Curry in the *Express*: 'Let no one under-estimate the importance of this victory, achieved as it was by the inspiration of Glenn Hoddle and Bryan Robson, the sheer industry of Sammy Lee and Gary Mabbutt and the bravery of Paul Mariner.'

Frank McGhee in the *Mirror*: 'England's midfield men formed the foundation of the victory with skipper Bryan Robson driving them on and little Sammy Lee and Gary Mabbutt covering every inch of the pitch.'

Glenn was given a free role that day in the Nep Stadium in front of myself, Sammy Lee and Bryan Robson. He was brilliant.

Two league games later I was badly injured in a tackle, playing at Stoke. I virtually did the splits and ripped my groin badly – it ended up as a hernia and put me out for three months. Any injury is unfortunate, but that one came at a particularly bad time for me as far as my England career went. Before it I had been making regular appearances in the national side and I felt I was making a niche for myself; since it, although I made a complete recovery, I have not been quite able to establish myself as an automatic first choice selection for England.

That said, I think I gave some of my best performances in an England shirt after the hernia. My first recall came as an over-age player for the Under-21 side against Denmark in Copenhagen – a match we won 1-0. Then came my reappearance for the senior team, against Yugoslavia in a

European qualifier, and one of my best ever games for my country.

I played in midfield in place of regular skipper Bryan Robson, and I scored my only full international goal. It was a header from a Glenn Hoddle corner and the tremendous feeling of soaring above the Yugoslav defence and seeing the ball in the back of the net remains with me to this day. There really is nothing like scoring for your country, and that in itself made the match memorable. The fact that we won 2-0 and went a step closer to the European Championship finals in West Germany made it even better.

I was also in the teams for the subsequent two qualifying matches, against Northern Ireland and Turkey respectively. We won the first 2-0 and drew 0-0 with Turkey, and then it came to the finals ... except that I was not selected. To have taken part in the qualifying rounds and not go to the finals was one of the most disappointing events of my career – ranking alongside my non-selection for the World Cup finals in Mexico, and definitely a huge let down.

Yet, I hope I can still retain my sense of humour with regard to the England scene. I'll never forget the day before the Wembley international with Hungry, not long after my debut against West Germany. We were working on set pieces in training. Bobby Robson called me over. 'Hey, Ray Mabbutt, come over here', he shouted. Now, my dad Ray had played 14 years for Bristol Rovers but never managed to make the full England side. I rang my dad that evening, and told him he was playing for England at Wembley, and to make sure he got an early night!

My aim to get back into the current full England squad was encouraged recently when Bobby Robson appointed me captain of the newly re-instated England 'B' team for a three match summer tour of Switzerland, Iceland, and Norway, exactly a year before the World Cup finals. As soon as we arrived in Switzerland, the England manager called a team meeting where he chose me as captain. I see this as a sign that I may get back into the squad-proper in time for the World Cup finals. There were a lot of new faces out there in Switzerland, I hardly knew anybody, so it was like being on my first England Youth trip many years earlier. For that reason we didn't start off too well in the first match after only one day's training together. Yet we still managed a good result, a 1-0 victory, and that was important because it was the only game Bobby Robson was able to see before going back to join up with the senior party.

It was very warm out there in Switzerland, but we were in for a dramatic change in temperature when we got to Iceland for match number two. This was my first time in Iceland and it felt as though we had landed on the moon, as we drove past lava-based mountain ranges from the airport to our hotel in Rekjavik. The temperature was well below freezing but some of the lads went off to a visit to a geyser, piping hot natural springs. The training took place on astroturf, and my Tottenham team-mate Gudni Bergsson was in the Iceland full international side. Although this was supposed to be a summer tour, it was bitterly cold come kick-off time and we only had short sleeved shirts. There was freezing rain two hours before the start and it persisted right the way through the game, together with a powerful wind. I have never been so cold in my life, as Miss Iceland led the two teams out onto the field. The ground was virtually empty, hardly anyone had bothered to turn out as the conditions were so atrocious. You can imagine how difficult it was to stand to attention and sing the national anthem with wind and rain lashing your face. We did everything we could to get warm, jogging on the spot, running up and down. Once the game started, as soon as the ball was kicked in the air, the wind would take it out of play. At half-time in the dressing rooms we all stood around with our teeth chattering. My hands turned blue with the cold, and my Spurs team-mate Paul Stewart was actually ill, with Chelsea's Tony Dorigo not too comfortable either.

My arms and hands felt four times their normal size. Just trying to talk was a problem. I remembered how cross channel swimmers cope with extreme cold by smothering themselves with Vaseline, or something similar, so I rubbed Vaseline all over my arms and legs. After about five or 10 minutes of the second half Paul Stewart couldn't continue. He was suffering from a mild form of hypothermia and had to go off. Somehow, though, we won the game 2-0. I was desperate to score back in the England fold, but was unlucky, hitting the bar with a header. At the end we all sprinted off the pitch, we couldn't wait for it to finish, and dashed to stand under the boiling hot shower to try to get some feeling back into our bodies.

Most of us recovered fairly quickly, even though we were all blue with the cold, but because of my diabetes my circulation is not so good as the other players' and my feeling didn't come back right away. The tips of my fingers suffered most of all with a mild form of frost bite and it lingered for the rest of the tour, and for six to eight weeks afterwards. But it was a consolation that Spurs have a branch of their Supporters Club in Iceland and they came to the team hotel to present me with their Spurs Player-of-the-Year award. Although we played the full Icelandic national side we were not awarded with full caps, as Bobby Robson made plain to us during his team talk in Switzerland. There had been much discussion as to whether it would mean a full cap, and in fact Steve Perryman won his only England cap the last time the national side played in Iceland.

When we moved onto Norway it was baking hot, so it was sunburn rather than frostbite with which we had to contend. We also encountered the best pitch of the three games and the toughest opposition, but we did alright once we kept out of the sun! Again we won and went back happy in the knowledge that in all three games we did not concede a single goal. Steve Bull scored a couple of times and that catapulted him straight into the senior England squad ... and he scored against the Scots at Hampden.

CHAPTER SIX

A FAMILY AFFAIR

I don't think it's an exaggeration to say that as soon as I could put one foot ahead of the other I had a ball at my feet. My father was a professional footballer with Bristol Rovers and one of my first memories is of becoming aware of this fact. With a bit of initial encouragement from Dad it didn't take long for Kevin (my older brother by two-and-a-half years) and me to become hooked on football, and naturally it didn't take much persuading to get Dad joining in!

I remember at the age of five or six hanging round outside the Bristol Rovers players' entrance, along with other autograph hunters, waiting for the home and visiting teams to emerge. When Dad appeared, however, Kevin and I stopped waiting for signatures and rushed to carry his kit bag ... one handle each. We definitely felt immensely proud to walk with him through the crowd of kids, knowing that he was not only our father, but also one of the team.

Growing up in what was undoubtedly a footballing environment was fun and never struck me as unusual or rarified in any way. When not at school Kevin and I were more often than not to be found outside with a football, and Dad frequently took us to a local park. Other children would be kicking a ball about somewhat aimlessly, but Dad had a more scientific approach – giving us different skills to practice by means of different exercises. He would work on our weaknesses; for example, we were both right-footed, so he concentrated on making us use our left feet to bring them up to the same standard. Also, neither of us is very tall (nor is my Dad) and we worked on timing and heading. This has made us better-than-average headers of the ball for our heights.

It would be wrong to imply that our every waking moment was spent in a football obsessed frenzy. I imagine I had a fairly 'normal' childhood, what with school and homework and so forth, and I certainly was never forced by Dad to practice or go out and play. My first junior school was Glenfrome and then I moved to Elmlea, which was where I really got into sport.

This enthusiasm continued, and was developed, at Cotham Grammar School, where I moved on to after the Eleven Plus, and I got involved in nearly every sport available. I played soccer (of course!), rugby, athletics, basketball, cricket, representing the school at most of them. Quite simply, I enjoyed sport. And it's part of my father's philosophy that playing several sports can only be a good thing. He didn't think I should necessarily stick only with football – I didn't – and he encouraged me in whatever I was doing.

However, that said, soccer emerged as the area I wanted to concentrate on and by the time I left school, a month before my sixteenth birthday, I knew Bristol Rovers were going to take me on as an apprentice. This took the pressure off me somewhat, as far as my 'O' levels went, though that wasn't to say the results were unimportant. That would have been a fairly shortsighted view, since it is as well to be prepared for the time when you can no longer play football. I did in fact gain my Maths, History, Geography and English Language 'O' levels and this would have enabled me to progress to the Sixth Form, had I not already secured the place with Rovers.

I think that if my football future had been less certain at the time I would have wanted to continue with my education on a full-time basis. I hadn't hated general school work and I certainly got a fair amount out of it. Again, my parents seemed to have had a balanced attitude, in that Kevin and I always had to do our homework before going out to practice any football. It was not assumed that an interest in sport automatically excluded any other interest, or any need for education.

My father himself had trained in financial planning whilst still playing professional football. One reason for this being that, at the time he was playing, the money was not particularly good; and another was to ensure he had something to continue to make a living by once the football stopped. Although footballers can now earn very good money indeed, there is still the moment when it stops and many have found that period difficult to cope with. I'd go along with Dad's view that it's as well to have an eye out to the future and, for this reason, firstly, to get a good basic education.

Still, there always comes a point where a decision has to be made and when this moment came I chose football. The family support and encouragement had been a constant factor in my life and because my Dad was from a footballing world it was easy for him to be part of that aspect of my life. He came to as many of my school matches as he could and would generally offer his comments afterwards. But he never preached. Even when Kevin and I both reached the high level of turning out for the Bristol Schools 10-11 age group, he remained quietly on the touchline, rather than shouting his head off.

He would point out what we'd done but, perhaps more importantly, what had not gone quite right and what still needed working on. It was valuable, not only for the advice, but also in teaching us to accept some criticism and comment. Even now, out of habit, I still ask Dad's opinion after a match, and he still offers it. Hopefully, though, he finds less to criticise now than when I was ten!

I remember when I was 11 I wanted us to have a colour TV and asked Dad about it. I didn't get a positive response – he thought it might take my mind off my school work. However, at the start of the school holidays, no doubt fed up with my constant nagging, he said he would get one ... provided I could juggle a ball 100 times on my left foot, 100 on my right, 100 alternating between the two, 100 on each knee and 100 times on my head! I was allowed a break between each discipline. 'If you can manage all that, I'll get you a colour TV,' he told me.

It took six weeks of practice, right the way through the summer holidays, but by the end I could do it. I called Mum out to witness my success and count the number of times I kept the ball in the air. We did get the colour TV and, as a spin-off, my skills had improved no end. This is just one example of how Dad managed to get us to work on our football without dictating or being overbearing about it and, crucially, making it fun at the same time.

I was recently reminded of this talent of my father's in an incident with my little sister Sally Anne. She was desperate to have her first bicycle and kept asking Dad about it. He said she would get one, but only after doing some tennis exercises which he thought up for her and which she could practice on the court he had built in his garden. She did them and got the bike – perhaps he's got plans for her at Wimbledon one day!

An interest which developed during my childhood, along with football, and which has stayed with me, is travelling. We used to go, as a family, on camping and caravan holidays all over the place. At first, when we were still young, we visited different places in Britain and then, as Kevin and I grew up, we extended our range to cover most of Europe. I remember being excited as we would set off for Yugoslavia – or Spain, France, wherever – stay at a couple of places on the journey and then settle for a couple of weeks in a spot my parents had picked out.

I have to confess that even when we were away from home we would still take a football, go out of a morning, and find a space to practice! Often we could find a local game going on, or a few other holiday-makers to join us, so somehow or other we managed to get our exercises done, whatever country we were in. I still very much enjoy travelling and football has taken me to many places in the world, from Europe, to the Far East and Australia. Now though, if I'm on holiday I go easy on the training, since most of the rest of my year is taken up with it!

One of the great inspirations to me in footballing terms, in addition to my father, was to watch the progress of my brother Kevin. Being a couple of years older than me, he was always just that bit further ahead in terms of different team age-groups, turning professional and so on. But we got along very well indeed, practised together and watched each other play. On occasions I travelled, with Mum and Dad, to Scotland and Holland, to see Kevin in action. Of course there was a bit of competition between us, but it never seemed to take over completely, to the extent that we had huge rows, or stopped talking to one another.

We both graduated at the same time in the Bristol Rovers juniors and a subsequent thrill for me was to go down to Wembley to see my brother play for England Schoolboys against France. The rest of the family came too and we saw Ken Sansom, Mark Higgins and Russell Osman alongside Kevin in the team. The crowd of 40,000 created a marvellous and exhilarating atmosphere which, at that young age, impressed me enormously. It was an emotional experience when I caught sight of Kevin as the teams lined up for the National Anthems. I felt tears of pride and joy rolling down my cheeks.

Kevin went on to turn professional with Bristol City. He naturally attracted a fair amount of publicity and was described as 'Kevin Mabbutt, son of Ray Mabbutt' virtually every time his name appeared in the papers. The family were quite well known locally and by the time I was getting media attention I was 'Gary Mabbutt, son of Ray and brother of Kevin'! This could have been seen as something of a problem: while it is well nigh impossible to emulate others in your family, it is also potentially difficult to gain a reputation of your own and escape their shadow.

As I see it though, it all comes down to how much you want something (in my case a career in football) for yourself – how much you put into it, not how much of a head start someone can give you. Had I been half-hearted about my football I might have resented my dad and Kevin and the collective shadow they cast over me and my attempts in the same game. However, being sure of what I wanted made it natural for me to appreciate what they had done, and to want to be part of it. In this respect, as in most, our family was very close and, inspite of my parents' divorce, really remains so to this day.

Kevin and I constantly came up against each other in school teams, with Bristol Rovers Boys and, when I was myself at Rovers as a professional, in City/Rovers local derbies. Although Kevin left Bristol City for Crystal Palace in a £250,000 transfer deal, I always thought that one day we would play together in the same side in the Football League. It was not to be. We did come close when Bristol City, with Bob Houghton as manager, made an offer for me at the time Kevin was there. That didn't work out, though, and I suppose it is one of my regrets, as I've always said that we would have combined well on the same side.

Another regret, of course, is that Kevin was forced out of the game through serious injury. He was an excellent goalscorer, with an outstanding record, but at the age of 26 he suffered a crucial knee ligament injury in a pre-season friendly at Southampton. He won't mind my saying that he was never one of the best tacklers in the world, and his attempt to win the ball going in hard rebounded on him as he fell awkwardly.

He suffered a terrible time in his bid to win back full fitness. As the elder of the two of us I think he had much more media and outside pressure on him to be successful, which is hard enough to deal with in normal circumstances, let alone when fighting for recovery. Of course any injured player always goes through torment when trying to save his career and livelihood, but I feel that for Kevin it was especially tough. He had so many more years ahead of him and had reached a stage where he had made sufficient impact to justifiably expect a big club move. He worked hard in rehabilitation, fought his way back and began playing again, but he failed to return to the sort of level of sharpness he had had before the injury.

I watched him in one game and could sense he was trying things that in the past he had been capable of, that had been quite comfortable, and which were now not coming off. It seemed that he was trying to come back too quickly, a mistake that a lot of players make in their understandable eagerness to return, and their frustration at having to be out for so long.

Kevin had actually done marvellously well to even resume playing at such a high standard, but he had lost a tiny bit and that is enough, at the top level, to make the difference. He left Crystal Palace for a spell in Canada, and then Cyprus, but his knee continued to play up until he was forced to consult a specialist. He then had to accept the inevitable advice to pack it in. It must always leave a bitter taste to go out of the game through injury, but Kevin has now got over the trauma. He has recently married and 'settled down', and works in the property investment business. He retains his interest in football, and comes to watch me as often as he can – another opinion, along with Dad's, to be sought after a match!

The third opinion that I seek on my football is, of course, that of my mother. She has now remarried but comes to matches as often as she can and remains as supportive and proud as she has always been. This support and belief was never more apparent than when I had been diagnosed diabetic. Obviously the whole family was hit by this news and I think it brought to mind memories of an earlier family trauma. This involved my younger brother Philip, who was born with spina bifida and who died just before his fourth birthday.

I recall Philip as a happy, cheerful child whenever he was at home with us – which was not often as he was in and out of hospital the whole time. One day the family, including my grandmother, went up to Sheffield and stayed in our caravan while Philip had to undergo a make or break operation. I remember being told that he had not made it through and although I was very young myself I still remember the devastating effect it had on the family.

Through Philip both my parents became involved with the Bristol and District Spina Bifida Association, and they keep up links with it today. When it was discovered that I had diabetes I'm sure they must have wondered why it was that these things seemed to hit their family, although they are both far too positive

63

to be bitter about it. At any rate, I hope that to some extent what I have achieved in football is a testament to my family's belief in me – it is certainly due in no little part to their encouragement and love.

CHAPTER SEVEN

CUP FINAL SURPRISES

The 1986-87 FA Cup final campaign had been a good one from my point of view, with a few goals taking us to the quarter-final stage against Wimbledon. No one in the Tottenham camp underestimated the task confronting us at Plough Lane, against one of the teams most difficult to beat in the game – when they put their minds to it! Immediately after the draw had been made the match was designated as the live TV cup tie on a Sunday afternoon.

The Dons went off to Spain to prepare for the match, while we spent most of the week leading up to the tie at a hotel in Brighton. Each morning we'd be reading the reports from Spain, with the Wimbledon lads eagerly predicting just how they would beat us. Glenn Hoddle was a particular target, and they were forecasting how they would stop him from playing. All this needle proved to be counter productive, because it really got our backs up and just made us more determined to 'show them'.

As it so happens when I joined up with the England 'B' squad many months later, I spoke with former Wimbledon goalkeeper Dave Beasant about it, explaining how those articles had annoyed the Tottenham players so much and had only succeeded in 'winding us all up'. He pointed out that he had been happy with the one article he had contributed, but that it was the headline which had caused friction. This had upset him, because it exaggerated certain points he had made, and he had had nothing to do with the choice of it.

There were plenty of TV pictures, as well, of the Wimbledon players expressing their determination to win, and pushing commentator Martin Tyler in the swimming pool to further enhance their reputation as the 'Dirty Dons'. But equally, there were plenty of determined forces working in our camp too, with our players fuelled up by the comments coming from Wimbledon, plus the motivating factor of wanting to get to Wembley for Danny Thomas. Danny had been badly injured in a match against Queens Park Rangers, and the manner of his injury had angered everyone at Tottenham. Danny should have played a big part in our team, instead he was fighting to save his career, which, in the end, proved an unsuccessful fight.

One incident which caused me to worry was the smashing up, by vandals, of our team coach. This occurred one night and woke quite a few of the players up – who then had a sleepless night. In addition to this, another coach had to then be found at very short notice.

However, we came through the match to strengьhen my belief that we possessed one of the best squads in the country at the time. We went to Plough Lane, refused to be put out of our stride, competed and finally got our reward. Glenn Hoddle and Chris Waddle scored brilliant late goals to take us through to the semi-finals. Immediately after the tough cup tie Glenn was interviewed live on TV and he dedicated his goal to Danny Thomas, who, we found out later, was in tears as he listened in his hospital bed after undergoing an operation on his damaged knee.

I felt a wonderful glow in the dressing rooms at Plough Lane. All of us were singing our hearts out in the bath for more than 30 minutes. It was an exceptionally satisfying victory.

For the semi-final against Watford at Villa Park we travelled to Birmingham on the Friday, after training. It was my first semi-final and all my family turned out. The atmosphere was simply sensational, with the Tottenham contingent occupying the whole bank of terracing behind the goal. The terraces were heaving with our supporters. It was the best atmosphere for a match that I had ever experienced – and, naturally, I was very nervous.

Watford had major problems, with their experienced goalkeepers Tony Coton (fractured thumb), and Steve Sherwood (dislocated finger), both ruled out. Eddie Plumley was the chief executive of the club and his eldest son Gary, a wine bar owner and part-time Welsh League player in Swansea, was rushed into the side for such an important game. However, there was no way we were going to be complacent just because we had a novice 'keeper against us. Sometimes a stand-in can produce a remarkable once-in-a-lifetime performance; he knows it will be his first and last game in the big time, and there is no reason to have any fear about it. For Gary Plumley it was a dream call up and I'm sure that even now he continues to consider it a dream.

For my part, I'm convinced it didn't matter who Watford had in goal on that day, the way we played we would have reached the final whoever it was. We were three up by half-time, and that is some going in an FA Cup semi-final. We got our fourth in the second half, and then they got a goal, but with only two or three minutes of the match left, I knew we had reached the final. My heart was racing and when the final whistle sounded I caught sight of Chris Waddle – he was crying. Our supporters were on the pitch celebrating. I know a lot of people have expressed the view that it looks stupid for grown men to hug each other, but I felt so emotional at that moment that I could perfectly understand the urge of 'grown men' to willingly hug each other! We stayed on the pitch for around 15 minutes lapping up and spilling out those emotions. I finally walked off wearing two hats, with three scarves draped round my neck. The TV cameras were in our dressing rooms, we were all in the bath drinking champagne – fortunately the one drink I'm allowed – singing 'We're On Our Way To Wembley'.

The excitement never stopped from that moment until we physically played in the final itself. The following Monday morning we were all in a studio recording a single with Chas and Dave, the song ended with the line: 'Danny, all the goals are for you'. That was my first time in the studio. A year later I was lucky enough to be in on the making of a record again – this time with the England squad for the European Championships. Stock, Aitken and Waterman produced the song and even though it turned out that I failed to make the squad for West Germany it was great to have been involved.

Time sped by in an adrenalin-filled haze of cup fever until suddenly Cup Final Day was upon us. We met up on Friday afternoon, had an hour's training at Cheshunt, and then left for the Ponsbourne Hotel in Hertfordshire. That was our usual hotel, although it had recently been taken over by Tesco and become their new management centre. Luckily, though, they allowed us the use of it for the Cup final. When we got to the hotel there was no mistaking the magnitude of the game the following day. The car park was jammed with TV units, the main entrance was decked out with blue and white ribbons and flowers. I started to get very nervous. We had dinner at the hotel, made some last minute phone calls, and went up to bed early at around 10.30 pm. I didn't think I would be able to sleep, but surprisingly I had no problem at all.

Cup final morning was taken up with scanning all the newspapers delivered to the rooms, the TV was on with saturation coverage of the Big Event on two channels. Even when it came to the Children's Programmes the presenters were all dressed up in Spurs or Coventry gear. Everything, it seemed, had stopped for the Cup final.

The players were interviewed by the hotel swimming pool, then came breakfast, followed by a stroll around the magnificent grounds and the pitch and putt golf course. I sat around the pool with a few players having a mid-morning cup of tea. There was more TV viewing and then a spot of light lunch.

It was simply an incredible feeling to be part of all the build up. We had a police escort guiding our coach to Wembley, more interviews on the way to the game, all of which took me back to the time when I was younger, sitting in front of the telly at home watching all the preamble to the Cup final. I had seen it so often I knew the TV format very well. It was a family tradition to have tea and chocolate biscuits at half-time, and when it was all over my dad, brother and I would go out into the garden pretending to be whoever had scored the winning goal! Now it was not make believe – I was there. I was being interviewed on the coach, a bit different from seeing it all from the other side of the screen.

Ossie Ardiles, Ray Clemence, Tony Galvin and I sat in the same places at the front of the coach that we had occupied on all previous rounds of the Cup. I suppose that was our little superstition. The route began to get congested, then packed solid, and once we turned the corner into Wembley Way the scene that greeted us was just a mass of Tottenham supporters. I had thought I was nervous before, but imagine how I felt when I turned that corner and caught sight of the Twin Towers and all our fans. I'd been to Wembley before. I'd played there for England. But nothing prepared me for the scenes that greeted us along Wembley Way.

The huge gates opened to let our bus into the dressing room area, and in the dressing rooms themselves our kit was all laid out. We strolled onto the pitch, looking superbly turned out in our smart club suits with button holes. The noise was tremendous when we came out of the tunnel – and it was still an hour-and-a-quarter before the game. The pitch was magnificent, it was a lovely sunny afternoon, and I stood there just trying to take it all in. I knew the spot where my family would be and I caught sight of them. All the memories flooded back about the time I came to Wembley with them to see my brother play in the England Schoolboy side. And now they were all there to see me!

The Coventry players were already out on the pitch and, as I knew their Chairman slightly, I went over and shook his hand. I must have given three or four different interviews at this stage on the pitch. It was not an inconvenience, in fact I wished that this hour-and-a-quarter would last for five hours, so I could have soaked it all up fully.

Back we went to the dressing rooms, changed, put on our Cup final track suits and were ready 10-15 minutes before the kick-off. As we stood in the tunnel waiting to come out, I felt the nerves of all the build-up over the five weeks, although knowledge of the way we had been playing helped to settle some of them. When we came out of that tunnel, I looked around and it was a mass of people, banks of them – the noise was deafening. I thought the atmosphere for the England versus West Germany international was something special, but the Cup final beat it. This was another of those moments I would wait for eagerly as a kid watching on TV. I would love it when they came out, and here I was doing it myself.

I began to relax once I saw my family and friends and waved to them. The Duchess of Kent was presented to the teams along with a number of dignitaries, and then came the National Anthem. There are some who believe that all the pomp and ceremony goes on far too long, but for me it's all part of the tradition of the Cup final and so needs to be preserved. I even enjoyed watching Rod Stewart and a team of celebrities play in a curtain-raiser to the final.

The two teams broke off after all the formalities and the two captains were called to the centre circle for the referee to toss the coin. The physios began collecting the track suits. It was now just a minute or two before the kick off as Chris Hughton turned to me and said: 'Look at your shirt, HOLSTEN is missing'. I looked down at my shirt and I couldn't believe it. I looked around at the team and Glenn Hoddle and I were among five of the players who had not got the name of our sponsors on our shirts! What can you do about that a couple of minutes before the start of the Cup final? You know there are 500 million people watching this game worldwide through the medium of TV and this is the sponsor's big day. There was bound to be panic at first until the realisation set in that the company would end up with more publicity over the mistake. In fact it would have been a sensational stunt had it been done on purpose as a PR idea.

We certainly put the shirts to the back of our minds pretty

70

quickly as we got off to a glorious start, the best start imaginable. The big Wembley pitch suited our style and a Clive Allen goal from Chris Waddle's cross came in the first few minutes. Then Bennett equalised very quickly after our initial strike. It was turning out to be one of the most enjoyable games I had ever played in and it pleased me that we were putting on such a good game at Wembley in the Cup final.

Just before half-time I scored. Our captain Richard Gough had gone forward for a free-kick and I was behind him. As the ball came across, he challenged the 'keeper and the ball fell past them both to me. I flicked it goalwards, with Coventry centre-half Brian Kilcline trying to block it. We both struck the ball at the same time, and I really didn't know what had happened until I looked up and was stunned to see it bounce into the corner of the net. The Wembley scoreboard then confirmed that Spurs had taken a 2-1 lead and my name flashed up as the scorer.

As I was leaving the field at half-time I was confronted by a TV interviewer who asked: 'Was it your goal?' I responded: 'I'll tell you afterwards'. I didn't want to talk about it while I had the game as a whole on my mind, but I was claiming the goal, there was no doubt about that.

There wasn't a great deal to be said by manager David Pleat during his half-time talk as everything was going well for us. He just stressed that he didn't want us to go off the boil. In the second half Keith Houchen scored a brilliant goal with a diving header to bring Coventry level again.

The match went into extra time, and in the first half of that we had a break through Mitchell Thomas. However, when our move ended, Lloyd McGrath sprinted down the Coventry right-wing into the gap left by our full-back. I ran back towards my own goal alongside their centre-forward, reaching the six yard box as the cross was struck by McGrath. I stuck my foot out and the ball hit me on the left knee. Nine times out of ten it would have flown out of play, but it was just my luck that this one time it looped up, and I could see Ray Clemence stumbling backwards, leaping as high as he could. It was no good, the ball

71

fell into the far corner of the net. It was a fluke, plain and simple. I found it hard to believe it had happened. I sank down onto my haunches, turned and gave Ray a sort of a smile as if to say I don't know how that could possibly have happened. Had it been a real error I would have been devastated to think I had scored an own goal in the Cup final, but it was a total fluke and I knew there was nothing I could have done about it.

There were still some 20 minutes to go and we tried everything we knew to get ourselves back into the game. When the final whistle went, the realisation that we had lost was a massive blow. The knowledge that we had lost to my own goal was not easy to accept. It seemed worse to me than losing a Cup final on penalties. I knew Coventry manager John Sillett and his general manager George Curtis from their days at Bristol City and Hereford, and I shook their hands. The Coventry players were jumping on top of each other in jubilation at overturning the odds and winning the Cup. When they came down to earth I shook them by the hand.

Very quickly I went to sit on my own in the middle of the park. I was inconsolable and didn't even see Coventry go up and collect the Cup, only realising they had received it when I heard the roar of their crowd. When their skipper Brian Kilcline raised the Cup a cold sensation came all over me, knowing that we had missed out. Our manager simply said that what had happened, had happened, and we should go up and collect our losers' medals. The Duchess of Kent handed them out and when it came to my turn she said: 'Congratulations, hard luck. I would like to thank you, on behalf of all of us, for all the good work you do for diabetics in this country'. I had just finished on the losing side in the Cup final, and had scored an own goal, but that was still very nice indeed to hear.

Down the steps and off on the lap of honour. I looked up at the family and shrugged my shoulders. 'What could I do?' As we're walking down the tunnel Ray Clemence was in front of me. I said: 'That's the first one I've chipped you all season!'

If a similar situation occured again, I would probably have the same response – to run back to try and cover. Although I didn't feel it was my fault, blame has to be apportioned, and my own goal got plenty of press coverage. But I felt that had we played to our full capabilities then we would have beaten Coventry on the day. All of our side played below par while the Coventry performance was magnificent. I've re-run the game on TV and in all honesty Coventry deserved their victory, all credit to them.

Nevertheless, that did not make the defeat any easier to accept. Numbness. That's all I felt as I sat in the dressing room immediately afterwards. Our dressing room was a sombre place, very quiet – everyone was totally dejected, no-one had anything to say.

We had a good team, an excellent one in fact, but we had nothing to show for what had been an exceptionally good season. We had finished third in the League, been semi-finalists in the Littlewoods Cup and reached the FA Cup final. But the biggest occasion in English football turned out to be a big let down for us.

We got bathed and changed, and I went to see my family who were waiting outside. As soon as I left the sanctuary of the dressing room I was besieged by about 20 members of the press. Naturally enough they wanted my version of the own goal that settled the final. I explained that I wanted to see my family first and promised to return fairly quickly. That satisfied them all apart from one who followed me out, but when I returned quite promptly the Wembley doorman refused him entry. A row broke out and a bit of a scuffle. Eventually he got in and a press conference was able to begin, lasting for 10-15 minutes. There were a lot of questions fired at me; my contract was up, I was going into hospital the following day for an operation and there were, of course, my two goals, one at each end. It was the first time that a winning goal in a Wembley FA Cup final was an own goal, the last occasion someone scored at both ends was Tommy Hutchinson for Manchester City against Spurs.

A massive marquee had been put up on the White Hart Lane pitch for the 'celebrations'. We left Wembley for our ground with the Coventry supporters clapping and cheering me on my way. There wasn't much to celebrate that evening, it was more about drowning sorrows in champagne. No-one felt like partying, but after a while Glenn and Chris got up on the stage and sang their 'hit' Diamond Lights, helping to put the smile back on our faces. The reality confronted us the next morning in the papers back at the hotel. We had lost. But we still had to fulfil our commitment to ride in an open-top bus, meeting up in Edmonton and travelling to a Civic Reception at Haringey Town Hall. En route a surprisingly large number of our fans turned up and there was one huge banner: 'DON'T WORRY GARY, WE DON'T BLAME YOU'.

Ironically the first game of the following season we played at Coventry. Minutes before the kick-off the Spurs fans began chanting 'There's only one Gary Mabbutt', and the Coventry fans joined in. The whole ground was echoing to my name.

As far as cup finals go, the UEFA Cup final was my first major one, but I only just made it. I had suffered a number of injuries throughout that season, missing the earlier rounds of the competition. For that reason I was one of the substitutes for the first leg of the final against Anderlecht in Belgium, although I came on for the final 15 minutes or so. Again there was a great atmosphere in a compact stadium. Before the game the streets were alive with Spurs fans and they gave us tremendous encouragement throughout the game. A draw was a great result for us, but it was tempered by the fact that our skipper Steve Perryman was booked and that ruled him out of the second leg.

All my family were at White Hart Lane for the second leg. European nights are special at Tottenham, a club with a marvellous European tradition. There is a particular atmosphere which ordinary League matches somehow fail to generate. I was selected for the team even though I couldn't kick with my left foot over long distances (I was to need a hernia operation immediately after the final).

Anderlecht went a goal ahead and Keith Burkinshaw put on both substitutes – Ossie Ardiles being one of them – and I came off. Ossie had a great chance after just a few minutes, but struck the underside of the bar from close range. I was sitting on the bench jumping up and down. When we eventually scored it was a great relief to everyone, even though it meant we finished all square and the final had to be settled by a penalty shoot out.

The tension was unbearable, having got so far in the tournament this was an unfair way of deciding the destiny of the UEFA Cup – or any competition for that matter.

I felt a little confident because of our goalkeeper Tony Parks. He was one of the best penalty stoppers I'd ever come across. He was always difficult to beat in training and, knowing that, I had a sneaking suspicion that it might go our way. It did. He saved two penalties and won the UEFA Cup for us. After the decisive save, I was the first to reach him diving on top of him, and then the others followed. There was a huge scrum. I was deliriously happy as this was my first major trophy success at the top level. It was certainly a proud moment when I collected my winner's medal and embarked on the lap of honour.

I was so pleased for Keith Burkinshaw and Peter Shreeve, but particularly for the former. We knew it was his last game as manager and we wanted to win the UEFA Cup for him. The look on his face told us how pleased he was to end his Spurs career on such a high note.

Our dressing room was packed with well wishers, and I hadn't a clue who half of them were. Later we opened all the windows in our room in the West Stand to give the fans a look at the trophy. The High Road was packed with our supporters.

We had a choice of London venues to continue the celebrations into the early hours but, personally, I preferred to go home with my girlfriend and family to open a bottle of champagne that I had in the fridge. I was more than satisfied with a quiet glass and the inner glow of winning my first major trophy.

CHAPTER EIGHT

MANAGERS

I have played under many well known managers, including Bobby Robson for England and Terry Venables for the England Under-21s as well as now for Tottenham. But my first manager as a 15-year-old schoolboy was Don Megson at Bristol Rovers. He was the boss at my very first pre-season training in professional football and it was a privilege, as well as a surprise, to inter-mingle with the first team players. It was Don's style to let the youngsters have a taste of the big time, making the lads feel important, even though he restricted it to the pre-season. I didn't get to know Don Megson too well, as the former Sheffield Wednesday player Colin Dobson, the ginger-haired left-winger, was in charge of the young players.

In my first season in the first team, Terry Cooper was player-manager with Bobby Campbell in charge. I liked Bobby Campbell for his honest, down to earth approach. He had been at the club for many years and was a great servant of it.

Next came Harold Jarman, taking over from Bobby Campbell, first in the capacity of caretaker manager, then manager. He was also a very loyal servant to Bristol Rovers and I had known him for many years before he became manager, as had most of the players at the club. In fact, he had played in the same Rovers team as my father. He was in charge when I was diagnosed a diabetic and I have to thank him for the way he reacted to the problem and gave me every chance to carry on in my career.

Terry Cooper was one of the game's really big stars when I was a youngster, so it was an honour to have such a close professional relationship with him, first when he was player-coach at Rovers, and then when he took over as manager. I had always admired him for what he achieved at Leeds, and also with England, as an attacking left-back. He was a great influence on me when I began playing in the same Rovers team because at that stage of my career, as a youngster, he was something of an inspirational figure. At the age of 17 one is very impressionable, and I was fortunate to have someone like Terry Cooper around to help, encourage, and guide me through some turbulent times. If I ever had any problems he was always available to talk to. That never changed when he became manager. I enjoyed first playing with, and then for, him.

Bobby Gould had spells with Rovers, first as a player, then as coach, and eventually he returned as manager. He had also been a player with local rivals Bristol City and was a big name, having played for several top clubs in his time. He was different from Terry Cooper in several ways – for a start he was strict with the young players when he began as player-coach at the club. I was an apprentice and part of our duties was cleaning out the dressing rooms, and cleaning the first team players' boots. The system was simple enough, the first team players would leave their boots hanging up in the boot room and we would clean them. Bobby Gould gave us instructions that anyone lazily leaving his boots in the dressing room should be punished. The apprentices would tie their laces in knots, as many knots as possible, to teach them a lesson. One day we came back after lunch to discover that Bobby Gould himself had left his boots lying around in the changing rooms. The older apprentices got hold of the boots and tied wicked knots in them, leaving them where they were. When he came in the following day to make his discovery, he was far from pleased and called all the apprentices to a meeting before the start of training demanding to know who was responsible. No-one owned up, so he picked on me. 'You did it ... it was you, wasn't it?' It wasn't me, but he ordered me to run a lap of Eastville Parks training grounds as punishment.

I suppose we had a love-hate relationship during his time there as coach and then manager. Yet I liked him as a player and even as a manager, and I suppose we got on quite well generally. We did fall out unfortunately toward the end of my contract at Bristol Rovers, when he wanted to sell me to Luton and I refused to go because the terms of the contract offered were far from satisfactory.

Keith Burkinshaw was my first manager at Tottenham and, in retrospect, I was lucky to have a boss like him for my first move into the big time. He was one of the game's real gentlemen, a Yorkshireman, very honest, down to earth, sometimes difficult to understand yet always straightforward and blunt. My first recollection of Keith Burkinshaw was after being introduced to him by Bill Nicholson at the training ground. I found our first talk extremely disconcerting, as he asked me what I considered to be my best position. I would have thought that at a club of Tottenham's stature and size, the manager would have done his homework on a new signing, but apparently he knew very little about me, which came as a bit of a shock. On the other hand, he was very forthright, explaining that I had only been bought as a squad player, and that if things went well he would call me into the team. Well, as it turned out I became a regular within four months, blending into the first team almost immediately. To me that demonstrated that Keith Burkinshaw was not a manager prepared to rely totally on reputations and also that he was a man of his word – because he had said he would reward me with a new contract if I made my mark in the first team. Although I had signed a three year contract and he was under no obligation, he raised my salary within months of my arrival at the club because I had made the breakthrough into the first team. He kept his word.

Under Keith Burkinshaw the club were highly successful. I

arrived after two successive FA Cup victories, and there was more glory to come. I felt that his partnership with Peter Shreeve was one of the main reasons behind that phenomenal success. They worked well together, Keith as No 1 and Peter as his coach, both involved in the training – a popular combination with the players.

Sometimes, though, Keith Burkinshaw could be a hard man to convince. After my first season at Spurs I treated myself to a summer holiday in Florida, at St. Petersburg Beach in the Don Cesar Hotel, a lovely pink-painted hotel right on the beach. I have fairly light coloured hair and I used a product called 'Sun-in' to enhance the lightness. When I came out of the sea I would spray it on my hair. But after two days it all went horribly wrong. I went extremely blond! When I returned home and joined up with the players for pre-season training, it did look as though I had been to the hairdressers to get this effect specially created.

The first day of pre-season training, Keith Burkinshaw called me over. 'My God, you've been here one year, had a bit of success, got in the England team, and typically you've gone all flash, dyeing your hair.' The boss had clearly thought it had all gone to my head, literally, and that I was off to Stringfellows every night, and going to the hairdressers to get my hair dyed blond. I was really taken aback by the way he saw it. I tried to explain to him how it had all happened. But he didn't accept it, feeling it was some sort of excuse and still convinced that I felt I was the bee's-knees. To make matters even worse, you can imagine the stick I took from the players. 'The Blond Bombshell', they called me. I left my hair and it took a season before the blond grew out and I was back to my normal colour. I certainly left hair colouring products well alone after that!

Despite the hair episode, I was very impressed by Keith Burkinshaw as man and manager. Obviously my allegiance would tend to be to the man who brought me to the club, but I still do have a lot of time for him. For a start, when I first met him he was honest enough to say it might take me two years to get in the side, but equally he said that if I was good enough I would be given a chance. Some managers stick steadfastly with their tried and trusted players. In fact, he showed such strength when Ossie Ardiles was forced to go on loan to Paris St. Germain because of the Falklands troubles. He re-shuffled the midfield and I became part of that department in Ossie's absence. I stayed in midfield even when Ossie came back, teaming up with him rather than being replaced by the Argentinian World Cup winner.

In my first season under Keith Burkinshaw we finished fourth in the First Division, and in 1983-84 we won the UEFA Cup in what turned out to be the manager's farewell season. Although there had been rumblings well before the end of the season that the manager would be out, I was surprised that he went. I had been sidelined through injury in the build-up to the UEFA Cup final, so it was no surprise that I was substitute for the first leg of the Final against the Belgian side Anderlecht. However, skipper Steve Perryman was booked in the first leg and would therefore, heartbreakingly, miss the second at White Hart Lane. As Steve had been playing in midfield the slot left available by his enforced absence gave both Ossie and myself a chance of playing. It was a straight choice between us and we were both only about 85 per cent fit. I had a hernia at the time, the legacy of an injury I got at Stoke, and could hardly kick with my left foot. It was a very tricky decision. Keith Burkinshaw had brought Ossie Ardiles over from Argentina, perhaps his most significant signing ever, and also got on very well with him personally. Yet, it was Peter Shreeve who was leaning more toward playing Ossie than Keith Burkinshaw. The manager wanted to deploy me in a man-for-man marking role on Anderlecht's danger-man Enzo Scifo, who had enjoyed such a good game in the first leg. At the time, Keith Burkinshaw knew he would be leaving the club and he was determined to go out a winner. In the end he picked me and Ossie was left on the subs bench, although he did come on in the latter stages of the final. I will always be grateful to Keith Burkinshaw for giving me my chance in my first major final.

Naturally, I was very disappointed when he left the club. It was such a shame because we had just lifted the UEFA Cup. Even though there was so much discussion at the time it was still very much a shock when he did leave. But, it was clear that he was fully aware of the position. I would have loved to have been involved in his testimonial match shortly after winning the UEFA Cup, and his last appearance as manager of a Spurs team, but I was in hospital undergoing a hernia operation. I telephoned the club and spoke to Keith, wishing him all the best. I suppose a player tends to get used to seeing managers come and go from clubs, but because Keith Burkinshaw had shown such confidence in me at vital times I was very upset to see him go. I was also very surprised that he failed to land a good job back in this country after returning from his stint in the Middle East. I thought he might have got the managerial job at Sheffield Wednesday before they appointed Ron Atkinson. On the other hand, one thing you learn in football is never to be surprised by anything!

I didn't have the same rapport with Peter Shreeve as manager as I did when he was No 2 to Keith Burkinshaw. Peter Shreeve succeeded Keith, and although I got on with him professionally, I always had this suspicion that I was not one of his ideal types of player. That view was only strengthened when he regularly dropped me from the team. Perhaps he felt he had good reason to leave me out because I had a succession of injuries at this time, including a nine week absence after a broken leg, and therefore always seemed to be fighting my way back from them.

In Peter Shreeve's first season as manager I spent a lot of my time on the substitutes' bench. There were times when we had disagreements, rather than outright rows, about my best position in the team, but having said that, he was very well liked by the players. His first season was excellent and we challenged for the championship, falling away only towards the end of the season. His second season slipped below the standards of his first, but I still feel it was unfair that any stigma should have been attached to him because of off-the-field events that occurred in Jersey. It was a particular shame that they appeared to contribute to his downfall.

The events took place during a pre-season tour in Jersey and started when some fellow tried to punch Clive Allen while he and a few other players were relaxing in a pub. Clive was then stopped for speeding and before we knew it the press had gathered on the island making all sorts of enquiries about our activities. The fact is that the whole episode was blown out of all proportion – easy to say, but I was there and that is the case. It was said that this incident started the rot, that it illustrated the lack of discipline within the camp, but I cannot accept that. As far as I'm aware, the reason Peter Shreeve was sacked was purely and simply because he failed to get the sort of results that would satisfy the board of directors and the supporters, particularly after such an encouraging opening season in management. It's a harsh fact, but in football if you start well you are still expected to get better, or at the least, match your previous performance. There seems to be no margin for error, or even adjustment, at the top.

When David Pleat took over at Tottenham, I've got to admit I felt a little apprehensive. My mind went back to the intriguing episode involving my former Bristol Rovers boss Bobby Gould and David Pleat, when Gould seemed determined to sell me to Pleat, and I refused to go because of the pitiful terms he was offering me to sign for Luton. In fact I had met Pleat a few times in discussions about that move and I knew he had become frustrated in his efforts to sign me, and of course I feared he might hold this against me when he arrived at White Hart Lane as manager. But all those worries quickly disappeared. If he had held a grudge it wouldn't have taken long to find out. I should imagine that David Pleat took my refusal to sign for him at Luton as part of the job of soccer management and I can guess that numerous players have turned him down in his time.

As it turned out I experienced one of my most enjoyable seasons at Spurs in David Pleat's first season in charge. He assembled one of the best squads in my time at the club, and all the players performed well at the same time. There was unity, harmony and it produced a team that finished third in the championship race, reached the semi-final of the Littlewoods

Cup – before going out to Arsenal on the narrowest of margins – and unfortunately finished up as losers in the FA Cup final to Coventry. Those achievements had a great deal to do with managerial ability.

I was very impressed with David Pleat as manager, and it was unfortunate that regrettable circumstances off the field forced him to resign. It appeared that he had no choice other than to resign after allegations about his private life. The pity of it is that he had built the foundations of a very good team. If he had been able to keep that squad together for another couple of seasons, adding to it as he went along, I'm sure it would have been capable of even greater achievements.

Two weeks before the first stories broke in the newspapers about our manager, I had signed a new five year contract. The Cup final was over, I had had an operation on my foot, my contract was up and I was involved in talks with a few top clubs. Eventually I signed a new long-term deal with Spurs. I then went off for a holiday in Spain where I bumped into Kenny Dalglish, to whom, ironically, I had been talking about a possible move to Anfield. The story about David Pleat reached us that very morning. I was walking along reading the front page article with incredulity and Kenny Dalglish could hardly believe it either. We avoided talking about it – it was an extremely embarrassing subject – but one couldn't help but feel sorry for the man. It never occurred to me at the time that these allegations would ultimately cause the demise of David Pleat as Tottenham manager.

My first thought was that he would be severely reprimanded by the club, which, of course, no doubt happened. I was obviously aware that as manager of such a big, powerful club, the only club on the full listing on the Stock Exchange, this sort of bad publicity would cause enormous problems, but I felt sure that he would be able to ride out the storm. However, when there was a second allegation the situation must have become intolerable both for the club and for David Pleat. Even so I still didn't think the repercussions would end with a resignation – there is so much that you read in the papers that turns out to be untrue, or, at the very least, exaggerated. But he resigned, and within four or five months the squad and the manager, who had done so well and looked to have such a bright future, had been disbanded. A month before his resignation he had appointed me club captain after the surprise £1.5 million sale of skipper Richard Gough to Glasgow Rangers.

Everybody within the club felt it was such a disappointment that all David Pleat's hard work had come to such an abrupt end. His coach Trevor Hartley took temporary charge, but his duration as manager was pretty brief, just a couple of weeks.

There followed a unique situation in football, a committee of three running the team; coach Doug Livermore, together with senior players Ray Clemence and Ossie Ardiles. I was not actually involved in the committee, in the business of picking the team, or any of the other team matters, but as club captain some of the players assumed that I must be. It was inaccurately reported in one or two papers that I *was* part of this selection committee and this caused friction in the dressing room. It just shows you the power of the media. One or two of my own team-mates began to believe that I was on the committee selecting the team simply because they had read it in the papers! The matter was brought out into the open when team changes were made. There was one player in particular who was far from happy because he had been dropped and he turned his frustrations on me, blaming me for the decision. I protested that it had absolutely nothing to do with me, but he was far from satisfied, far from convinced.

There were a couple more players who were so sure that I had a say in team selection that they came to me, to question me about it. They seemed to think that I might have something against them – of course, this was just not the case. The system of running the team by committee, with all the uncertainties it created about the input from other people such as myself, only served to create unrest within the dressing room. This totally unsatisfactory situation prevailed for several weeks until the arrival of David Pleat's successor.

Terry Venables had surprisingly been released early in the

season by Barcelona and Spurs moved in for him. The club tied up the deal when chairman Irving Scholar dashed out to Florida where Terry Venables was on holiday. It was clear that the club had pulled out all the stops to get him. Terry's record was impressive, first in this country with Crystal Palace and QPR, then winning the Spanish Championship in his first season with Barcelona and taking the club to the European Cup final in his second year. Everyone in the Tottenham dressing room was eagerly awaiting his arrival. But it was a traumatic time to take over – make no mistake, the club was in a state of turmoil. Terry Venables was hailed as some sort of Messiah. But, in reality, it was nonsense to expect him to wave a magic wand and put everything right. Even so, because of his great reputation, the moment he walked through the front door the atmosphere began to change.

Unfortunately in football everyone is a judge, an expert, and wants overnight success, immediate results. First, Terry Venables, along with everyone else at the club, suffered a humiliating FA Cup defeat at Port Vale. These sorts of things can happen and I would not blame the manager for it, it's really down to the players. His first season, or what was left of it, was a strange – almost limbo-like – time, and the start of his first full season was even worse. The opening match was called off at the last minute on the orders of the police, because construction work on the East Stand made it a hazard, in their view, for the spectators. On top of that, the Football League deducted two points for the club's failure to fulfil its opening fixture, and that sent us to the bottom of the First Division. The club, manager and players, became the butt of numerous jokes. One national newspaper published Spurs jokes each day for a week, and the rest of the media were on our backs. That would have been fair enough if the team had been badly organised, but that was not the case.

Some of the reports concerning our matches were an absolute disgrace, a complete distortion of what actually occurred, and this really upset us all. Certain players became targets, and the level of abuse was becoming unacceptable –

affecting families, particularly parents. Before Christmas we were being written off as relegation fodder. Then, after Christmas, we put a scintillating run together and the second half of the season proved to be the time when the Tottenham transition began to take shape. We finished up sixth in the table, quite a respectable position considering that we were once bottom. Naturally, the two points reinstated after an appeal helped to boost morale and put our league position in a truer perspective.

Terry Venables is a players' manager, and is great dealing with his team. Even when he was personally under fire from the media, when things were going so badly wrong at first at Spurs, he handled himself magnificently. He is a very high-profile manager, and when it was going wrong for us as a team, that rebounded on to him. But, he always kept his cool, despite a very difficult situation. He was never rushed into any panic measures. He retained total commitment to, and confidence in, his players. A lot of managers would have made a signing or two just to keep everyone happy. Terry Venables only bought when he wanted to, not because he was forced to. Some will criticise him for some signings, maybe they will say the price was too high, or whatever, but the fact is that a major reconstruction job was needed after the FA Cup final against Coventry when that team and its manager David Pleat disbanded.

Ray Clemence and Ossie Ardiles came to the end of their illustrious careers, while Richard Gough had been sold before Terry Venables arrived, and then Steve Hodge, Nico Claesen, Johnny Metgod, and Chris Fairclough were sold off. Glenn Hoddle was a special case, wanting to go abroad, and the club rewarded him with a transfer to Monaco a year before his contract expired, while Clive Allen came to the end of his contract, leaving by choice.

The manager needed the best part of a new team. Every manager I've played for has his own style and wants his own type of player. Obviously not everyone will agree with the manager's choice, but he will have his reasons for wanting a certain type of player. Apart from all the players Terry Venables has signed, there have been an awful lot more linked with the club in the media. At a big club like Spurs you get used to picking up the paper and virtually every day seeing who we are going to buy and who we are going to sell.

Terry Venables was to be seen every day on the training pitch with his assistant Allan Harris (until, of course, the latter departed for a job in Spain). He takes most of the training and the coaching. He is so knowledgeable, has an abundance of ideas on the game, and his innovations are first class. He is at ease with people – the media and the directors – and can get his message across to the players.

Some managers have problems in communicating with their players, but that's not the case with Terry Venables. He achieves this subtly at times, sometimes simply. He is not a ranter or raver, never losing control of his emotions. Still, if a player needs a corrective kick up the backside, he will get it, but Terry will do it his own way. When things were not going well, the manager did not feel the need for many team meetings or any 'here we go' gee-up talks. There was no need for the players to hide around corners fearing the fireworks and dreading being slaughtered in front of their team-mates, the method of some managers. Terry Venables is nothing like that, he is cool, calm and collected, sorting out precisely what needs to be done. It is significant that when he first arrived at the club he called all the players in for a meeting, and struck up a fine relationship with all of us immediately.

An illustration of Terry Venables' talent and shrewdness as a manager, was his signing of Gary Lineker. When Gary Lineker was sure the time was right to leave the Nou Camp, and when he decided that he wanted to return to English football, Spurs was his first choice – one of the main reasons for this being that he wanted to play for Terry Venables again. The acquisition of Gary Lineker provides the Spurs squad with a real depth of talent, similar to that of Liverpool. It's this sort of quality player, incorporated into a squad of 14 or 15 top line players, that enables a club to win the major honours. For example, last season Liverpool were able to sit players of the calibre of Ian Rush and Peter Beardsley on the substitutes' bench.

Every manager I've played for has used me as a utility player and Terry Venables is no exception. Bobby Campbell at Bristol Rovers was the first to tell me 'your best position is centre-half'. This may be so, but for the good of the club I don't mind playing in different positions occasionally. However, I do feel that centre-half is the best position for me, and it is certainly the role I feel happiest in.

Terry Venables' arrival at Spurs was not the first time I had played for him. In fact I first knew him when he was coach to the England Under-21s, and I was very impressed with him then. He is out of the same school as John Cartwright, a coach for whom I have a lot of time and respect – and who worked under Terry Venables at Crystal Palace.

However, as far as the England set-up goes, Bobby Robson is the main England manager I have played for. I might have played for him at club level but, as I understand it, he was reluctant to sign me for Ipswich because he was concerned about my condition as a diabetic. As I've already mentioned, he was not alone in having such fears. But thankfully he certainly did not worry about picking me for England. He gave me my big chance with the full England team and for that I will always be grateful to him.

He is a down-to-earth man who creates a good atmosphere within the England camp. The players are relaxed and happy, as the manager enjoys getting along with all of his squad. He has developed a sound working partnership with coach Don Howe, which has matured over the years. I feel that the England team is developing along good lines at an important time in World Cup year. There is some exciting new young talent emerging through the ranks, such as our own Paul Gascoigne and also Nigel Clough. It is important that all the potential is channelled in the right way, and in saying that I am referring not only to Gazza, who has attracted the bulk of the publicity. Any young talent requires nurturing and there are times when we all need advice as to how best to use our energies. By the time the finals come around in Italy I am hoping England will put out a very strong team and have the back-up of a powerful squad. I feel confident that Bobby Robson will parade a superior squad to the one he took to Mexico when we reached the quarter-finals, going out to Diego Maradona's 'hand-of-God' goal.

The backbone of that Mexico side has survived, with skipper Bryan Robson (so badly handicapped by injury in '86), Gary Lineker (the World Cup's top scorer in Mexico), Peter Beardsley, Terry Butcher, Chris Waddle and Peter Shilton. Such experience will be vital and to complement it there are some highly promising youngsters coming through. It is still my aim to be part of this squad and I hope I might be able to force my way back into the reckoning with some good early season performances in 1989-90.

CHAPTER NINE

THE MEDIA

Traditionally the working relationship between the media and the footballing world – players and managers in particular – has been somewhat uneasy. Although never ideal, it has perhaps been just about acceptable in the past, but that has now changed. Unfortunately things have reached an all-time low and are getting worse. Such deterioration is a worrying factor inside the game and urgently needs to be redressed.

I certainly accept the argument put forward by the media in this country that players are not as readily available as they are in the States, where the dressing room is open for interviews on virtually any subject. It is much the same in France, as I've been told by my old team-mate Glenn Hoddle in Monaco. Here, the press sometimes stand out in some atrocious conditions, hanging around waiting to grab a hasty word with a player or two. To a degree I sympathise with the way they are sometimes treated like dirt. That must surely be reflected in the way they write and report the game, which can be extremely aggressive, but there is nevertheless no excuse for what amounts to defamatory articles.

The working press seem to be split between those who concentrate on the actual sport, the reporting of the action, and those who are more concerned with what goes on *off* the field of play. Perhaps they feel that what goes on behind the scenes has now become more exhilarating than the football. It is also annoying that they concentrate on what is going wrong, tending to ignore what is going right – an imbalance that deeply frustrates those inside the game.

Personally, I've always had a good relationship with the press. I've never really been one to constantly demand cash payments for special interviews, although I have had plenty of opportunities. Instead, I'm more than prepared to make myself available for interviews – I've never turned one down and trust that I have answered any questions in the right manner, with due responsibility to the club and to the image of the game as a whole. That has been my philosophy even before I was appointed Spurs club captain. Certainly as Spurs skipper I feel it is my duty to make comments to the press on behalf of the players, if I'm asked to do so. Because I provide what I would consider to be adequate cooperation, I expect something in return. I don't think anyone can blame me, therefore, when I am attacked in articles, to such a degree that I am convinced it is detrimental to my character and career, for taking retaliatory action.

One article written about me came as a total shock because it just materialised right out of the blue. In fact, I was enjoying myself on holiday in Portugal when someone, who had obviously recognised me, came over, stopped me in the street and said: 'I see you want to leave Spurs.' I was totally taken aback and really didn't quite know what he was talking about. Naturally enough I asked him to explain, and he informed me that he had read it in the newspaper out there. It wasn't easy to obtain a copy of that daily paper in Portugal, but I managed it. I also rang home to see if the story had been repeated in any of the other newspapers, but fortunately it had not. The article was full of untruths and misrepresentations; it said that I had one year left on my contract, but at that time I actually had three years remaining; and it suggested that I had told friends that it was time for me to leave Tottenham, which was simply not the case. It also went on to suggest that the club were willing to cash in on me at that time rather than wait for my contract to lapse and risk a fee being set by the Independent Tribunal.

It just seemed to me that the basic journalistic principle of checking the facts was missing here, and that the result of such a piece in a big-selling national newspaper would be a rift between me and the club. That concerned and affected me so much that it ruined the last four or five days of my holiday. All I wanted to do was to get back home and sort it all out with the club. I actually telephoned Tottenham from Portugal, anxiously trying to speak with manager Terry Venables. He wasn't at White Hart Lane so I spoke to coach Doug Livermore, explaining that in no way had I said anything to the paper or to any so-called friends.

But I really needed to talk with the manager as the article stated that Terry Venables had rejected all bids for me, intimating that possibly Spurs would sell me if the price was right. It is easy to imagine that my mind was racing until such time that I returned home. Even so, I knew that my relationship with the supporters would be strained, and perhaps my relationship with the club might be damaged as this article hinted that I was involved with it in some way, which, of course, I was not. If I were a Spurs fan and I had read that article over my breakfast cereal my reaction would be 'some player that Gary Mabbutt, saying he wants to leave the club and he is supposed to be the skipper setting an example.' I feared that this article would be a sure-fire way of getting the fans on my back.

It wasn't long before my fears were realised. When I got back I discovered that the club had received numerous calls about this and my mail bag was full. I even got some letters at home. Some were abusive, but I have kept one which I felt was fairly balanced and typical of the response. Clearly, people had believed what they had read, and who could blame them?

'Dear Gary Mabbutt,
I know two kids who know some people who live near you, this is how I found out your address. Lately in the newspapers there have been stories that you might be leaving Tottenham. Hopefully that's not true.
Spurs are one of the best teams in the country and they

are on the edge of something really big next season. The Spurs team we have at the moment is one of the best in the first division. If we lose you, nobody could replace you as a defender or as a captain. You're the best Spurs defender and you should also be in the England team.

Please, please, please, please, please don't leave Tottenham. They're the best.

Could you please send me back something showing whether you will be leaving?'

There were so many letters on the same subject that it was almost impossible to answer them all. The best way I could respond was with some quotes in the Evening Standard putting my point of view: I didn't want to leave and had no intention of pushing for a move at all.

The irony is that if I had decided to sue the paper that started it all off I would have been on a loser. Quite simply, it would take more than a year to get to court and by then anything might have happened – I might have been transferred!

Seriously, I heard that something like that once occurred, when Queen's Park Rangers sued a newspaper which said that Michael Robinson was being sold to Liverpool. At the time the article appeared the West London club were adamant that there was no intention whatsoever of such a transfer. They began the legal proceedings, but about six months later the player was sold ... to Liverpool! That's why one has to be so careful before entering into any litigation.

It seems to me that the gap between the media and football is getting wider, and it is about time something was done to bridge it. There needs to be some controls, some mechanism for setting down a code of conduct. There needs to be a great deal of discussion – giving and taking – between the Football Writers' Association, the Players' Union, the League and the clubs.

I do not believe that the present system, whereby some top name players are paid for 'signed' articles, is satisfactory. Often I have refused to take money from newspapers in exchange for putting my name to an article. The problem is that these 'signed' pieces are getting out of hand. There are many well known figures who have left the game, as well as those still involved, who are eager to go beyond the realms of acceptable criticism and into sheer character assassination, revealing a dangerous and destructive streak which really cannot be justified. These people know who they are, they don't need me to name them, and I'm just amazed that they need the money so much that they would sell themselves and their good name. They should think, think about their victim's wife and family, his mum and dad. I'm sure some of these so-called 'paid' critics would have shuddered if they had been the subject of this level of abuse from their peers of the past. How would they feel had Stanley Matthews torn them to shreds in front of millions of readers? I've no doubt they would have been heartbroken and, quite rightly, aggrieved.

Unfortunately, chequebook journalism is a fact of life and, with agents involved, it is something that will not change. How can you blame agents for asking for payments for their clients when there are so many papers prepared to pay? In my view the fault lies with papers which make too much money too readily available. Clubs try to impose bans on their players to restrict such activities, particularly if they bring the player or the club into disrepute. But even this fails to work, because players are just human beings and if there is big money being offered they will understandably be tempted to take it. Some players may be on big salaries, but they have short careers and they will take as much as they can while they can to protect their families and secure their futures and who would blame them for that?

Yet, those players who do contribute pieces have to take the risk that the newspaper they write for one week may, the following week, slaughter them. Then, they have little comeback because they have taken the money and must, in turn, accept the 'stick'. When a player accepts money, he must also accept this possible development. However, that does not give the paper the right to make changes to an article to make it more effective, more eye-catching, and therefore a better 'sell'. The problem is that a paper is only really interested in the 'juicy' bits, the scandal. I'm sure that 60 per cent of the country believes that players are only interviewed when there is payment involved. The fact is that not every player talks to the press only if money changes hands. The fact is that the vast majority of interviews are conducted without payment, notably in previewing games and after matches.

Another disturbing aspect of the current trend is the headline writer, usually an anonymous 'being' locked away inside a newspaper office that people in the game don't know, never see, and never hear of again. In many cases the headline barely reflects the contents of the article. I have had personal experience of how a headline can completely distort an interview.

It was the summer after our Cup final defeat by Coventry, and my contract with Spurs had expired. I was involved in talks with a few clubs including Manchester United but, as we know, I decided to stay with Spurs. It was a coincidence that in the early part of the new season Spurs were playing at Old Trafford, and I was approached by a sports reporter on a national daily newspaper for an article he said he was planning to write leading up to this match. I told him of the respect I had for Manchester United, and indeed Liverpool and all the clubs I had talks with that summer over a possible move, but that I was very happy in my decision to stay at Tottenham. I added that I was delighted by the interest shown in me by a club of the stature of Manchester United. I couldn't have been more complimentary to Manchester United.

Yet, when I picked up the paper over breakfast on the morning of such a high-pressure first division match, I was greeted with a double page headline that screamed. 'UNITED MEAN NOTHING TO ME.' I was angry. A few hours later I had to go out and face them. As you would expect, I was 'crucified' by the United supporters even before the game started. I was booed during the warm-up! One man had sat in his newspaper office writing his headline and it resulted in

Photo: Action Images

Scoring for England against Yugoslavia, November 1986. Viv Anderson third from left, Terry Butcher far right
Photo: Action Images

Celebrating with Terry Butcher (second from left)
Photo: Action Images

Chasing Norman Whiteside of Northern Ireland, April 1987

Photo: Allsport

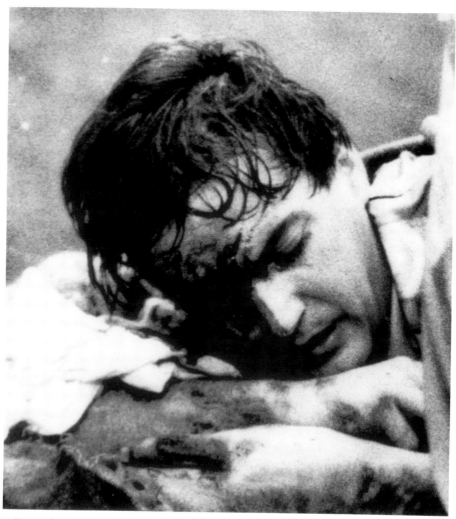
December 1987 – being carried off the pitch at Derby after a severe clash of heads
Photo: Daily Mirror

The resulting scar from that injury
Photo: Monte Fresco for the Daily Mirror

Still carrying evidence of the head injury, in the form of my headband, in a match v Oxford, March 1988
Photo: Monte Fresco for the Daily Mirror

Beating Arsenal's Alan Smith to the ball

Out-jumping Paul Parker of QPR, November 1987
Photo: Action Images

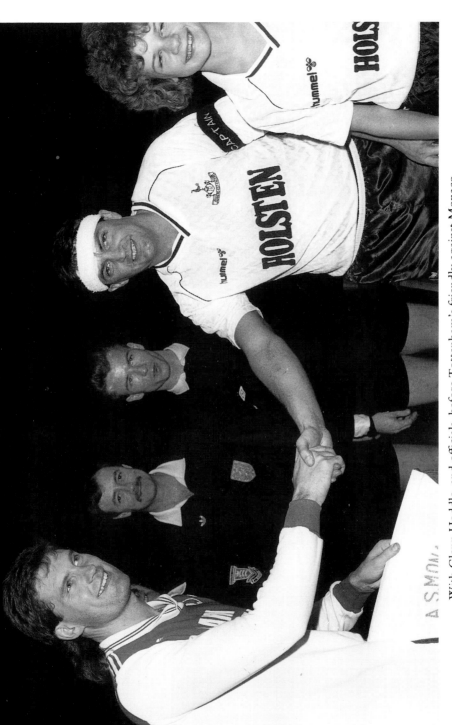

With Glenn Hoddle, and officials, before Tottenham's friendly against Monaco,
February 1988
Photo: Action Images

Presenting Chris Waddle with his Spurs' Members' Player of the Year Award 1987–88
Photo: Action Images

On duty for the British Diabetic Association – receiving a donation from Kevin Ratcliffe, on behalf of Everton FC

Photo: Action Images

Best Man and Groom – before the wedding of my brother Kevin in the summer of 1989

Wedding group outside the church, including our little sister Sally-Anne (front right)

Photo: Action Images

40,000 people baying for my blood. Yet, had the headline adequately reflected my sentiments, they might have been cheering me!

The easy way out for a sports journalist is to complain that the headline wasn't written by him and therefore he should not be held responsible for it. I cannot agree. I feel that each journalist should be responsible for the headline that appears above his article. Of course I accept that a sub-editor can drastically alter the whole meaning with just one paragraph cut for the sake of expediency, resulting in a perfectly good article becoming totally misleading or even inaccurate. However, in this instance the sub-editor should perhaps be more alert to the damage he can do. Either way, responsibility for the consequent article must lie with someone – journalist, sub-editor, editor – and it is this responsibility which seems occasionally to be shirked.

Football cannot do without the press, and likewise the press cannot do without football. I don't moan when the press say what a great player Gary Mabbutt is, or that he should play for England, in fact I love it and so do my family, but neither do I moan if I am criticised for having a poor game. All I ask for is a fair deal, fair criticism – that I can accept.

The trouble is that the press are all too keen to build up a personality or an outstanding talent only to knock him down again, and then build him up again. Paul Gascoigne is the perfect example. The press will say he is good for the game, a joker, a laugh, a real discovery and the sort of character sadly missing from the game ... then, wallop, they will knock him. I'm convinced that a few papers only sent their reporters on the England 'B' summer tour because Gazza was there, and he is always newsworthy. If he had not been in the squad, they wouldn't have gone. From my point of view I feel it is all wrong that papers have covered such a tour to follow just one player, rather than taking an interest in the matches. We won all three matches – in Switzerland, Iceland and Norway – but the actual games hardly rated a mention in the national press.

I do not want to give the wrong impression, as I feel the

media have a valuable part to play in the way the game of football is projected to the fans and the public at large. For example, I hope the way the media have portrayed my particular set of circumstances would have helped many people come to terms with their diabetes. The media have contributed in my aim to get a message across from the Diabetic Association to a lot of those afflicted, and their families, about how they can lead a normal life. The media, I am sure, helped push my cause towards fulfilling my ambition to play for England when they suggested that I was a potential future full cap after my performance for the Under-21s in Denmark, in front of the new England manager Bobby Robson.

Whatever the ultimate rights and wrongs, I still feel that the common view of a professional footballer has been sadly and sordidly distorted by the media. Certain sectors of the press promote an image of the professional footballer as someone who generally says he is 'sick as a parrot' when anything, no matter how slight, goes wrong. The image is of a man with no brains, who spends the majority of his spare time in Stringfellows, when he is not kicking a ball around or driving a big flash car. The media are guilty of building and projecting such an image and it is not a helpful one for the majority of us footballers to have to deal with.

The truth is that players are far more aware of their responsibilities than ever before. The Professional Footballers' Association (of which I am a committee member) has become one of the most powerful voices in the administration of the game, while the behaviour of its members is of paramount importance to its secretary, Gordon Taylor, who is often put forward as a potential leader of the game as a whole. However, if there are 280 players with the interests of the game at heart, it only needs one 'bad' character to spoil it all. Players have to learn that their responsibilities are to the game. Yes, it's great fun for the crowd, and good for the game, when larger-than-life characters who also have talent, emerge. But – and it is boring to reiterate this, but true nevertheless – football is a team game, a one-man-team just would not work. It is when people realise how to integrate their individual skills into a team that football really takes off, when they see that they can enhance the team by their play and through that, the image of the game.

It is up to everyone, the players, the clubs, the administrators, *and* the media to work in the same direction.

CHAPTER TEN

ROOM-MATES

I suppose the best way to get to know a fellow professional footballer is to share a room with him! To combat the monotony of long tours and away trips players tend always to share rooms – the company helps pass the time and goes some way to solving the problem of boredom. A single room would mean spending countless hours by yourself.

In my time I have been fortunate to have shared a football field with some of the best talent this country has produced. I have also had the honour of sharing a room with some of them ...

When I arrived at Tottenham as a young lad from Bristol Rovers, taking my initial steps on the big First Division stage, Steve Perryman was skipper of the club. He was one of the best captains in a long line of outstanding ones at Spurs. It is no surprise to me that he has gone into management after finishing his illustrious career as a player. His name was synonymous with Tottenham Hotspur and he was an enormous influence both on and off the field at the club. He was the perfect professional and, for a young man such as myself, seeking advice, he was the ideal person to consult. He was unfailingly helpful to me.

I shared a room with him on only one occasion – his usual room-mate being goalkeeper Ray Clemence. However, during this particular European campaign (1983/84) the former

England 'keeper was not in the side and Tony Parks had taken his place in goal. The night before the vital second-leg tie at White Hart Lane, Steve and I chatted in our room, watched TV until around 10.30pm and then went off to sleep – or, in my case, tried to go off to sleep.

I'm a very light sleeper and Steve had warned me before we teamed up for the night that he was prone to snore ... occasionally! He assured me that it was a light snore – but that night he must have had a cold or something, because I just could not get off to sleep for the sheer volume of noise. I tried my best to nod off, I really did, but at around 2am I had given up the ghost. I'd had enough, although I naturally still desperately needed some sleep. So, I wrapped a towel around myself and, as quietly as I could, sneaked out of the room, down the stairs to Reception and got myself another room for the rest of that night.

The following morning Steve had obviously noticed that I hadn't been around all through the night, but he chuckled when I told him why I had had to leave him. The routine for an evening match like this European tie would be to train in the morning and sleep in the afternoon. Fortunately Steve slept like a baby in the afternoon – not a peep out of him – so at least I got my rest then.

That was the first and last time we roomed together, as we resumed with our normal partners for the next match. I can't really complain too much about Steve, or any of my other room-mates for that matter – afterall, they have all had to watch as I've injected myself. They have all looked after me, been concerned that I ate the right amounts of food, made sure there were plenty of sugar lumps or chocolate around the room in case I ever went 'low'.

John Lacy was the first room-mate I had when I joined Spurs. He was an established professional at the time and I was his apprentice, so to speak – running around for him. I even made his tea in the room and served him with biscuits. We shared for a year, until he was transferred to Crystal Palace, and we have remained firm friends – and, coincidentally, neighbours – ever since.

102

Steve Archibald was an outstanding player for Spurs, one of their all-time greats. His touch, control and awareness, particularly in front of goal, were remarkable. At his peak he was one of the best strikers in the country and certainly among the best I have ever played with.

There can be no question of Steve's value to the team on the field, but there has been a great deal said and insinuated about his influence off it. Personally, I got on with him very well indeed, but I have heard it said that he did not get on with the other players and was a disruptive figure within the dressing rooms. He definitely liked to do things his own way, was very single-minded in his attitude and could be somewhat introverted. As a result, some people interpreted his behaviour as standoffishness. There were those within the dressing room who resented the way he was and his style could rub people up the wrong way.

An example of this was arriving at the team hotel for an overnight stay and Steve refusing to go down to dinner with the rest of us. He simply felt like a snack rather than a big dinner, so he would have something sent up to his room. As far as I'm concerned that was his choice and he should be respected for it, but some of the team found it an irksome attitude and one which they saw more as a reaction to themselves, than as a trait of Steve's character. In fact, I would go so far as to say that perhaps this singlemindedness and ability to be himself was one of the things which helped make Steve the player he was.

Whatever his relationship with some of his team-mates, Steve's rapport with the Tottenham crowd was wonderful. They adored him. 'We'll take good care of you, Archibald, Archibald' they would sing at every match he played in. Amongst the players of the last decade he would have to be counted with Glenn Hoddle and Chris Waddle as the crowd's favourites. His fellow players, too, respected and admired him for his sheer footballing ability. With Garth Crooks in the early 1980s he formed the most lethal goalscoring partnership in the game.

Perhaps sometimes a little too much is expected of individuals in terms of conformity and 'being one of the team' in what is, admittedly, a team game. Naturally a football team spends a great deal of time together; pre-season tours, away trips, match days, training and so forth. At times such as Christmas, when most people expect to be with their families, we are with each other. For this reason some of the players like to have a bit of a break from the rest and Steve was one such player. I can't see that this is wrong or that it should be denied them.

Of course being in a team means that any friction tends to be magnified and it can be a very fine line indeed between being perceived as a valid, and valuable, individual team-member, and an aloof, superior one. For me Steve was definitely in the former category.

Rooming with Tony Galvin has to be classified a fascinating experience – for one thing, he must be the only footballer with a PhD in Russian. I shared with him for three years, longer than any other player, and we really got along well together. Although he now plays his football at Swindon, Tony and I remain close friends and see each other regularly.

He's a typical Yorkshireman – a very dry humour – and it was never boring sharing a room with him. We used to have discussions on a wide range of topics, including politics, the treatment of people, current affairs and, even, football! There was only one problem. On occasion, like Steve Perryman, Tony snored. Usually it wasn't too bad: I would either shove a pillow over his head, or slap him on the back, both of which actions caused him to stop.

The real difficulty as far as Tony was concerned was getting up in the morning. I tended to be out and about quite early, about 8.30am, but not Tony. He wouldn't (or couldn't) get out of bed till 10am. He never wanted breakfast, which was just as well as he'd usually missed it anyway, and I had to sneak out of the room to get mine so as not to wake him. He was very grumpy if his slumbers were interrupted and, as a rule, was pretty tetchy until his first cup of tea. I used to tell him: 'I pity your poor wife, having to put up with your moods first thing in the morning.' Normally, I would get back from breakfast, put the kettle on and make him his tea – to ensure the best mood possible when he finally woke up.

As for his footballing prowess, Tony was one of the club's unsung heroes, rarely getting the kind of praise, recognition, or attention his role in the side thoroughly deserved. He played on the left-hand side of midfield, fulfilling an incredibly complex function, in both attack and defence, that required an enormous amount of commitment and dedication. He performed this role to perfection.

Although we shared a great many interests, including a love of books, we did not share the same appreciation of music: he hated all the music I liked and vice versa. In fact, such was the impossibility of finding an artist we both liked, we frequently both sat in our room listening to our own cassettes through our own Walkmans!

With Chris Waddle this was never a problem – we shared musical tastes and could listen to one music system in the room. We first were room-mates on England Under-21 duty in Scotland when I was still at Bristol Rovers and he with Newcastle. I was very disappointed to see Chris go to Marseille last summer (1989), even though it was obviously the chance of a lifetime for him. I know when he first arrived at Spurs he found it very difficult to adjust, particularly with the crowd getting on his back, but he eventually won them over with his exceptional football ability. Each year he got better and better until, in his final season, he was our most outstanding player.

For myself and for the team I would prefer him still to be around contributing to our effort, and it certainly came as a complete surprise when I heard he was off to join Glenn Hoddle in French football. I was on holiday in Spain when I learnt the news. Walking along the sea front with a few friends, a news-stand caught my eye and I saw a huge backpage headline referring to Waddle's move to Marseille. I had never had even an inkling and when I saw the fee was more than £4 million I was staggered. It was incredible.

However, in one way the fee explained the move, since I was sure Spurs had been reluctant to sell Chris and that he would have been reluctant to go. Still, that amount of money made it a good deal for both club and player and one which both parties would have been considered foolish to have turned down. If Spurs had stood in Chris' way, he would have been a very disillusioned, unhappy player, losing out on the biggest financial opportunity of his career. Equally, I knew he relished the challenge of football on the Continent, of being able to pursue every player's dream of trying to win the European Cup. In four years with Spurs he had yet to play a European cup tie of any description and the European experience will be vital to him in a World Cup year.

Having pointed out how good the transfer deal was for both Chris and Tottenham, I must say that I can't help but think that the loss of Waddle had weakened our team. After his best season for the club I wanted him to stay around and so did the rest of the squad – not to mention the fans. We were all looking forward to seeing how Chris and new signing Gary Lineker would combine, and with Gazza maturing we felt we had the foundations of a really good and exciting team. I think that the Waddle/Lineker combination would have had a major influence on our season. Still, that is now not possible, so we have all had to readjust and look at a different set-up.

Not only did Spurs lose a great player in Chris Waddle, but I lost my room-mate of one year. We were sharing at the turbulent time of David Pleat's departure from Tottenham and, as two of the senior team-members, had ample opportunity to discuss the situation as well as our playing form. We stopped sharing with the arrival of Paul Gascoigne, as it was felt, naturally enough, that the youngster might settle in quicker with a fellow Geordie – they spoke the same language for a start!

I also roomed with Mitchell Thomas for a year and can report that he is one of the quietest sleepers I've shared with. As we are both still single and live quite close to each other it fitted in well to be room-mates. Mitchell is a lively character, very bubbly and rarely down, even when left out of the team. He takes it all in his stride – or in the bath, which is where he seems to spend most of his time! He locks himself away for hours, even reading in there.

In my view the acquisition of Gary Lineker was the biggest transfer coup of the season, particularly considering the amount of money involved – about £1.3 million. I was sure he would leave Barcelona for another top foreign club – perhaps in Italy, or a wealthy club like Monaco. With so many of our top internationals being lured abroad it was gratifying that Gary returned to these shores after three highly successful seasons in Spain. He has shown his quality over the years, notably finishing top scorer in the 1986 World Cup Finals in Mexico. He is also one of the most popular players in the country and his arrival at Spurs helped convince me that we are getting a squad together which is capable of challenging for top honours.

The first thing I asked him when I knew we would be rooming together was whether he snored! He said no, he was a silent sleeper, which was reassuring. The first trip we shared a room was our 1989 pre-season tour, which included visiting Norway. Poor Gary immediately had the unnerving experience of seeing me go 'low' – which must have made him wonder what he'd let himself in for. It happened after the match and the subsequent meal and disco. Gary got back to the room ahead of me, as I had decided to walk. On my way I could feel my sugar level going down, but before doing anything about it I chatted with Gary.

As we were talking our Norwegian international 'keeper, Eric Thorstvedt, phoned up from the hotel lobby. I answered the call and, I later discovered, was extremely rude to him. 'Don't bother us,' I snapped, among other things. As usual when going 'low' I had little control over what I was saying and doing. In fact, I was falling about the room and Gary thought I must be drunk – completely legless – and he couldn't believe this sort of behaviour from his new skipper and room-mate. What's more, to really convince him that I was the worse for drink, I burst into song, blasting out my rendition of Gloria

Estefan's *1-2-3-4 come on baby say you love me*. Then, off came my jeans and I carried them round the room as if they were my dancing partner.

Next came a knock on the door and in came Eric. Just like Gary, he felt I must have hit the bottle hard. Once again I was rude to him, before leaping on to the bed and beginning to exercise, swinging my legs up in the air. As both Eric and Gary were new to the club neither of them was fully aware of my true condition. I'd had one glass of wine all night, although it hardly seemed like it to them! They became concerned about my behaviour, naturally enough, especially when I kept saying 'no, no, I'm, low'. I was very vague about what was going on and they didn't have a clue.

However, there are always lots of chocolate bars in my bag and I quickly munched my way through three of them. Within 10 minutes I was right as rain, except that my shoulder was extremely sore where I had been falling against the walls. As I recovered, I told Gary what had been happening and explained my condition. He then told me how rude I'd been to Eric – which was very embarrassing for me to hear. I guessed that Eric would tell the rest of the players how drunk and abusive I'd been, so next morning I apologised to him and filled him in on my particular details. There are times with diabetes when you end up doing an awful lot of explaining!

Three players whom I've never actually roomed with, but who I rate among the best I've ever had the privilege to play alongside, are Glenn Hoddle, Ossie Ardiles and Richard Gough. There is no-one to touch Glenn Hoddle for sheer ability. I firmly believe that he should still be a major influence in the England squad as it prepares for the next World Cup and am slightly concerned that he doesn't seem to be. I feel he's been left out a bit too early. His move to Monaco, in my view, has only enhanced his experience and ability to make an impact in international football.

He can provide the sort of passes that Gary Lineker and Peter Beardsley need. Not that I'm saying there are no other midfield playmakers in English football who can fulfil that function, but

Glenn has exceptional ability that really needs to have special attention. The one time that England played a midfield specifically to accommodate Glenn it worked a treat. That was in Hungary, where Bryan Robson, myself and Sammy Lee allowed Glenn the freedom to express his skills behind two strikers, at the head of midfield. On that day Glenn was magnificent, scoring from a free-kick and creating another goal in England's 3-0 victory. Obviously it's a shame that Neil Webb has such a bad achilles injury, but I wouldn't hesitate to bring Glenn back into the squad to replace him. I'd love to see him back in the England set-up, but have to say that I don't think it will happen.

In training Glenn was a sight to behold – his ability with the football seemed limitless and no one could match him. He is simply the most gifted player I have ever played with, or against. Not only that, he is also a great person off the field – always taking time to talk to and help youngsters – and I will always have a lot of time for him.

You can't help but like Ossie Ardiles, he's a terrific character and I was always very close to him. I didn't like golf too much, and still don't, but once Ossie took it up he insisted that I try it too – his enthusiasm was infectious. He became fanatical about it and roped John Lacy and myself in to accompany him on numerous rounds. I was usually the one struggling. Ossie picked the knack of the game up very quickly and I was the one trudging around looking for lost golf balls.

Another of his great passions was chess. He would loan me his computer chess system, and I could just about manage a game against the lowest level – in contrast to his being able to outwit the most advanced one! Still, I did develop a bit of a taste for it and manage to fit in the odd game now and then.

Ossie seemed to have an aptitude for most sports, including tennis, and he was certainly a magnificent footballer – the most superior foreign player to have played on these shores, in my opinion. It was ironic that I actually joined Spurs to replace him when he was forced to switch for a year to Paris St Germain on loan, because of the Falklands War. I wore his No 7 shirt for my first season at Spurs and it proved a lucky shirt for me as I established myself. When Ossie returned I played alongside him in the No 6 shirt, which wasn't too bad either.

Scottish international Richard Gough and I forged the best central partnership that I have enjoyed at the club. It was a shame that he was transferred to Glasgow Rangers, but the £1.5 million was a phenomenal fee which Tottenham could hardly turn down at the time. From my point of view, I would have loved it for Richard to have stayed, he is such a good quality defender and would only have got better. We both liked to go forward and I remember in one game we both got caught out of position, leaving a gaping hole, although usually we organised it so only one of us went forward at any one time. Despite Richard's being in Glasgow, we keep in touch regularly.

Finally, I must mention Bryan Robson, although there is very little I can say about him that has not already been noted. He became my regular room-mate in the England squad and he is undoubtedly one of the most important figures in English football over the last decade. It is significant that whenever he has been unfit and unavailable for the England team there has been a crisis atmosphere – illustrating just what a lynchpin he is. I don't think it is possible to overestimate his influence on, and importance to, our national side.

CHAPTER ELEVEN

HILLSBOROUGH

The disaster at Hillsborough touched the hearts and souls of everyone in the country. No-one will ever forget it. Merseyside's mourning for the 95 who perished on the Leppings Lane terraces has been the grief of a nation.

It was my duty to be in Liverpool just nine days after Hillsborough to attend the funeral of a Spurs fan who died at that Liverpool–Nottingham Forest FA Cup semi-final.

To actually be in the City of Liverpool, filled with such sorrow and anguish, at that time really brought the tragedy home. It was a painful experience, but it was also one I was glad to undertake. To make some contribution, no matter how small, was worthwhile.

Saturday April 15 1989 was the day of Britain's biggest sporting tragedy. The horrors were vividly brought into our homes by the power of television. The shocking sight of the chaos and subsequent loss of life will stay in people's minds for a very long time. TV brought the Bradford fire into our living rooms and the 39 deaths at Heysel, but somehow the images of Hillsborough seemed more vivid, closer to home, even more frightening.

However, even though the TV screens were filled with morbid scenes of death and the agony of the bereaved, there is still a crucial distance between the viewer and the event shown. On Friday April 21 that distance, for me, vanished.

Kenny Dalglish's secretary had telephoned Terry Venables' secretary with a special message for me. Liverpool Football Club wanted to let me know that one of the boys who had died at Hillsborough was in fact a Tottenham fan – not only that, but I was his favourite player. The family requested that, if it were at all possible, young Andrew Sefton had wanted to be buried in one of the Tottenham No 6 shirts that I had actually worn during a game.

My response, through the secretaries of both clubs, was, of course, 'yes'. In fact, I offered any other assistance either through the club or as an individual, and I suggested that the club should be represented at the funeral.

The next day Spurs played Everton at White Hart Lane. An emotional game. Our fans brought the spirit of Anfield to White Hart Lane and the gates were draped with scarves, flowers and messages. It was as if part of the Anfield shrine had come to Spurs, and it was touching to see. The tributes remained undisturbed on the gates for days after the match as a fitting memorial.

There was a one minute silence before the game with Everton, the first Merseyside team to play after the disaster. No-one broke that silence at 3.06, the exact time the semi-final had been halted in Sheffield.

Just before the game we were told that the funeral of the young Spurs fan would be on Monday at 9.30 am. It was decided that I would be attending. The club also sent a letter of condolence to the family and a bouquet of flowers to the funeral.

It was still dark when I set off from my Hertfordshire home on Monday morning for Liverpool, arriving at 9 am. Among the mourners at the Church were Phil Thompson and Terry McDermott representing Liverpool FC.

Outside the Church I spoke with Phil and Terry, as well as members of Andy's family and also the priest, who asked me whether, because I was such a firm favourite of Andrew's, I would read the bidding prayer.

It is hard to explain my feelings on the steps of the Church. From a purely personal point of view, I felt almost honoured that somebody I had never even met would have wanted me to say prayers for him. Honoured is almost the wrong word, I can't find the right one. I suppose I felt that in a very small way I was contributing something positive amidst all the devastation. You can never bring someone back, but you can hold them in your memory with love and respect. I felt proud.

It was hard to imagine just how upset people were, just how much they had suffered, until I experienced it for myself at such close range. It brought back memories for me of my younger brother who died because of spinabifida when he was only three. I was about seven at that time, but I well remember the devastation that caused in our family. I knew how much the family of Andrew Sefton were suffering.

On the steps to the Church Andrew's father grasped my hand. He held it tightly for two or three minutes. He told me how his son had been a great admirer of mine, and he thanked me very much for attending the funeral. Andy's fiancée was clearly trying to recall the good times and the good things about Andy. 'Every time you appeared on TV, he would give you a cheer', she told me.

'Even when we got engaged, Andy told me the only reason was "you have legs like Gary Mabbutt" '.

The service was sad and ended with the hymn Abide With Me.

On Friday April 28, I received this letter:

'Dear Mr. Mabbutt,
May I, as one of Andrew Sefton's best friends, give all my thanks to you. I was a pallbearer at his funeral which you attended on April 24. Your speech was excellent and I'm sure our Andy would have been very proud to know you've even mentioned his name. As you could probably appreciate we did not have time to thank you personally. I went to the match with Andrew and was lucky to get out

113

unhurt. Andrew will, though, never be forgotten and neither will the presence of his favourite player. Once again Gary, thank you on behalf of me and all of Andy's friends.

'Yours sincerely,

J. Quinn.'

The depth of the mourning on Merseyside had been brought home to me. Andrew Sefton's death and the deaths of the other 94 must not have been for nothing.

Here was a soccer-mad lad who had gone to this match because of his deep love for the game. The shrine at Anfield, and the one at White Hart Lane, demonstrated the feelings of supporters from all over the country who were united in their grief and their respect for each other. Those feelings surely cannot go to waste. They are important. Football has been brought closer to the community at large and those within the game have been brought that much closer together in the realisation that soccer grounds must be made safe.

I was in favour of bringing down the fences. They are cages that show the fans no respect. But, in their turn, the fans must respect the clubs' decisions to tear down the cages. Remember why they were put up in the first place – to prevent idiots invading the pitch. If this act of faith in the fans is misplaced after Hillsborough it will not only be a crying shame, it will mean that the clubs brave enough to take down their fences will have to put them back up.

Had there been no fences at Hillsborough, lives might have been saved.

A tiny minority of fans brought about the need for fences, the need for segregation, the need for video cameras, and all the other anti-hooligan measures. The needs and interests of the majority shouldn't be ignored simply because of this minority.

Evidently a solution needs to be found, one which curbs the desire of some fans to invade the pitch, whilst at the same time not preventing enjoyment of the game and not being a death-trap. Not easy to achieve, I admit. But there are some electronic fences which have been used successfully abroad, notably in France, and perhaps clubs here might employ them. Certainly it seems to me that all-seater stadiums are part of the overall solution – some 'atmosphere' may be lost, but not much, surely, if the soccer lovers still keep coming?

The game cannot put the clock back, but it can learn from Hillsborough to ensure 95 people didn't lose their lives in vain. It must never happen again.

CHAPTER TWELVE

THE FUTURE

My burning ambition is to get back into the England squad.

The biggest disappointment in my career to-date has been my failure to be selected for the World Cup in Mexico and for the European Championships in West Germany.

I am convinced that I can still play a major role for my country and am just waiting for the call. My target is the 1990 World Cup finals in Italy. To achieve this all I can do is my best; keep working, keep playing, and keep on improving. I am only 28, not the age to be written off for the international scene. I believe that if I play well enough the England manager will not forget me.

At the start of season 1989-90 there were about three years left on my Spurs contract, I'm settled at the club and I'm convinced that Terry Venables is on the threshold of producing an outstanding side. I know it's often assumed that if a team is doing exceptionally well then an individual will be more easily spotted by the national manager. However, I firmly believe it is down to the performance of the individual – so it is up to me to be effective and consistent.

Although I'm known as a versatile player, I have been holding down a regular place at centre-back. When David Pleat took over as Spurs manager, it looked at one time as though he would definitely sign Terry Butcher from Ipswich. I would have liked Terry to have come to Tottenham as I wanted to play alongside him. I wanted to forge the England central defensive partnership of the future by playing regularly with him in the same league team. I'm sure we would have combined well together and who's to say we wouldn't still blend well for England?

Terry came close to signing for Spurs. He had detailed and prolonged talks with the club, but eventually he chose Glasgow Rangers. I'm sure he is happy with his choice and he has certainly enjoyed enormous success at Ibrox.

As it turned out David Pleat signed Richard Gough, my predecessor as skipper. The best partnership I've had on the pitch has been with Richard. The team had an outstanding 1986-87 season, third in the First Division, semi-final of the Littlewoods Cup, where we lost so narrowly to Arsenal, and then the famous FA Cup final defeat to Coventry.

My last game for England was against West Germany in Dusseldorf at the start of the season before the European Championships. I know the England manager was bitterly disappointed with the 3-1 defeat. He must have been exceedingly upset with certain individuals and I can understand that.

Nevertheless I still harboured hopes that I would go to West Germany for the European Championships. I played in two of the qualifying games, against Northern Ireland and Yugoslavia at Wembley, and had been a regular in the squad. It seemed as if the England manager was toying with the notion of taking a versatile player such as myself, but in the end opted to have cover for virtually every specialist position. Chelsea's left-back Tony Dorigo went, I didn't.

That was my second big set-back with England. Perhaps the worst was not making the cut for Mexico in 1986. This time the England manager did take a cover player ... Gary Stevens. Good luck to Gary, he's a smashing lad and recently has suffered so much through injury. I didn't begrudge him the pride and pleasure of representing his country in the World Cup finals.

But, I must be honest and say that I thought it was going to be me. I had made a full recovery from injury and Bobby Robson came to watch me at Luton before naming his squad. I won the man-of-the-match award marking Mick Harford, a centre-forward I have always found awkward to play against. The press were convinced that after that performance I had booked my ticket to Mexico. It was a big shock to me when I missed out. In fact I couldn't believe it.

Of course, all players think they are good enough to be chosen. But, in my case, I don't believe I've ever let the England manager down, and I'm sure that he doesn't think that I have. I still feel, deep down, that my England career is not over. Certainly Bobby Robson has not told me that he would not pick me again. Then again, he hasn't told me that he would! He is not obliged to say anything to me. But I feel I have played well whenever he has come to White Hart Lane and hope I can play well whenever he sees me in the future.

Bobby Robson has always struck me as an honest, open and fair man. I do not believe for one minute that he holds anything against me personally. In fact, he was big enough to pick me for England, even though as a club manager with Ipswich he had wanted to buy me, but changed his mind.

As it turned out I owe him a lot. He was the one who picked me for England almost immediately after taking over as national team manager. I have always found him likeable, both as man and manager, and certainly do not approve of the personal attacks he and his family have been forced to endure lately at the hands of the media.

The only way any England manager is going to be successful, in the media's eyes, is by winning the World Cup or the European Championships. Bobby Robson is amenable and accessible to the press, yet he still gets crucified if the slightest thing goes wrong. In my view it has become a personal vendetta by some papers, particularly those conducting telephone votes on whether he should be sacked or not.

At one time there was even a series of Robson jokes, which I didn't find funny. We at Tottenham had to suffer the jokes ourselves at the start of last season (1988-89) and we found the only way to put a stop to them was by winning. To his credit, Bobby Robson has come through all that very well. He has retained his dignity.

Season 1989-90 is obviously a big season for everyone with ambitions to play for England in Italy ... which, of course, includes me. I'm not big headed enough to say that I feel I should be in the England team, but I do firmly believe there is a place for someone who can play a variety of positions. That I have done for England. I would like nothing better than to be going to Italy with Chris Waddle and Paul Gascoigne. Both Chris and Gazza have the talent to be major successes in the World Cup finals.

Gazza ... well, what can you say about him? Bobby Robson was right when he said he is daft as a brush! But he is also a brilliant, exceptional talent. His skill has to be carefully nurtured. He needs his abundance of energy guided in the right direction – he requires discipline. He will get the guidance he needs at Tottenham under Terry Venables and both club and country will benefit. He has all the talent, but he has yet to gain the experience to go with it. In contrast, Chris is seven years older, and seven years wiser, and will benefit from his move to Marseille.

Still, you can't help but love Gazza, and everyone at the club has his own favourite Gazza story. Mine is the time when he was getting some stick in the *Daily Mirror*, accused by an irrate photographer of being greedy for supposedly demanding money to be snapped with DJ Bear as a promotional stunt. In the dressing rooms the next day the boys were giving him some stick about it, then we all went out training, while Gazza was held up having his leg strapped.

He ran out after us with a £50 note stuck on his forehead! He trained, rushing about, kicking the ball. He did everything with that £50 note stuck to his forehead, and he never said a word or even laughed. They say the characters have gone out of the game. Well, here is a genuine character alright.

The crowd love him, and it's easy to see why. He is a crowd pleaser and the game needs its entertainers. There are so few genuine talents and characters around, I'm all for him doing his

120

thing, so long as the team lose nothing because of it. He has to learn it is a team game. When Bobby Robson said that the England players wouldn't put up with him larking around when the chips are down, I can understand it. I'm convinced that he will learn, though, and Gazza will become a very, very big name over the next few years.

For the moment it's Chris Waddle who can make the bigger impact with England, inspite of his staggering £4 million-plus move to Marseille. Once he had a torrid time with England, booed by the Wembley fans, finding it difficult to justify his place in the team. Now he has emerged from that and become a cornerstone of the team, in my view. He is taking on more responsibility, and his talents are really beginning to shine through.

In a transitional season, Terry Venables' first full season at Tottenham, Chris was our outstanding player. But there has been a huge gap in his soccer education. He missed out, like so many, on the European scene for his club. Now he will be gaining invaluable experience in the European Cup with his new team, Marseille.

I know I gained immeasurable experience from Spurs' European campaigns and particularly reaching the UEFA Cup final. Our biggest let-down is the continuance of the European ban. There can be no doubt it has held some players' development back, and that in turn has started to have its effect on the national team. There are only a handful, such as Gary Lineker when he was at Barcelona and the England players at Glasgow Rangers, who have European experience.

I still believe that English football supports one of the strongest leagues in the world, but we have been hit so badly by the ban on our clubs in Europe that it showed up in the England team's performances in the European Championships in West Germany. Once our clubs are back playing in Europe I'm sure we will see the benefit at both club and national levels – and I hope very much to be a part of it all.

STATISTICS

**Compiled by Andy Porter
and with thanks to Mike Jay**

International career

Gary's international career began soon after his 18th birthday when he was selected for the England Youth Team to take part in the Yugoslavia Youth Tournament. Along with his Bristol Rovers team-mate Paul Petts, Gary played in each of the four matches, scoring two of England's four goals. Later in the 1979-80 season he played in both the UEFA Youth qualifying matches and rounded off his 11-cap Youth career with a UEFA Youth Tournament winner's medal in East Germany. He played in all three group fixtures plus the semi-final and final. His 11 Youth appearances were:

1. 9.79	v	W Germany in Pula – drew 1-1
3. 9.79	v	Poland in Porec – lost 0-1
5. 9.79	v	Hungary in Pula – won 2-0 (scored once)
8. 9.79	v	Czechoslovakia in Pula – lost 1-2 (scored once)
31.10.79	v	Denmark in Esbjerg – won 3-1
26. 3.80	v	Denmark in Coventry – won 4-0
16. 5.80	v	N Ireland in Arnstadt – won 1-0
18. 5.80	v	Portugal in Rosslau – drew 1-1
20. 5.80	v	Yugoslavia in Altenburg – won 2-0
23. 5.80	v	The Netherlands in Halle – won 1-0

25. 5.80   v Poland in Leipzig – won 2-1

Nearly two years later Gary gained the first of six England Under-21 caps, three of which were won after his 21st birthday. Each of the six matches was in the UEFA Under-21 Championship which England won in 1982 and 1984, but he did not play in either final. The Under-21 matches are:

17. 3.82   v Poland in Warsaw (QF 1st leg) – won 2-1
 7. 4.82   v Poland at West Ham (QF 2nd leg) – drew 2-2
19. 4.82   v Scotland in Glasgow (SF 1st leg) – won 1-0
21. 9.82   v Denmark in Hvidovre (Qualifier) – won 4-1
              (scored twice)
28. 3.84   v France in Rouen (QF 2nd leg) – won 1-0
12. 3.86   v Denmark in Copenhagen (QF 1st leg) – won 1-0

Earlier this year (1989) Gary added to his tally of England 'B' caps when he captained the team in each of their three tour matches. His only goal at 'B' level came with a glancing header in the last minute of his debut at the City Ground, Nottingham. His England 'B' games are:

13.11.84   v New Zealand in Nottingham – won 2-0 (scored once)
16. 5.89   v Switzerland in Winterthur – won 2-0
19. 5.89   v Iceland in Reykjavik – won 2-0
22. 5.89   v Norway in Stavanger – won 1-0

After just four Under-21 appearances Gary made his full England debut and on only two of the 13 occasions listed below did he fail to play for the full 90 minutes. These were against Luxembourg in 1982, when he was replaced by Glenn Hoddle 15 minutes from time, and versus Scotland in 1983, when coming on as a substitute for Bryan Robson after 24 minutes. Eight of his full caps have been gained in European Championship qualifying games, three in British Championship matches and two in friendly fixtures.

13.10.82	v	W Germany at Wembley (friendly) – lost 1-2
17.11.82	v	Greece in Salonika (Eur. qualifier*) – won 3-0
15.12.82	v	Luxembourg at Wembley (Eur. qualifier) – won 9-0 (substituted)
23. 2.83	v	Wales at Wembley (GBC**) – won 2-1
30. 3.83	v	Greece at Wembley (Eur. qualifier) – drew 0-0
27. 4.83	v	Hungary at Wembley (Eur. qualifier) – won 2-0
28. 5.83	v	N Ireland in Belfast (GBC) – drew 0-0
1. 6.83	v	Scotland at Wembley (GBC) – won 2-0 (came on as substitute)
12.10.83	v	Hungary in Budapest (Eur. qualifier) – won 3-0
12.11.86	v	Yugoslavia at Wembley (Eur. qualifier) – won 2-0 (scored once)
1. 4.87	v	N Ireland in Belfast (Eur. qualifier) – won 2-0
29. 4.87	v	Turkey in Izmir (Eur. qualifier) – drew 0-0
9. 9.87	v	W Germany in Dusseldorf (friendly) – lost 1-3

* – *European Championship qualifier*
** – *British Championship match*

Several club-mates, past and present, have played alongside Gary at international level: Ray Clemence, Glenn Hoddle, Chris Waddle and Clive Allen in full internationals; Steve Hodge and Graham Roberts at full and 'B' levels; Paul Gascoigne and Paul Stewart in 'B' games only; Paul Walsh at Under-21 and Youth levels; Gary Stevens and Richard Cooke in Under-21 matches and Paul Allen and Terry Gibson in Youth fixtures. With Paul Petts, Gary became the first Bristol Rovers player to be selected for the England Youth Team since Steve Catley in 1970. He was also the first Bristol Rovers player to gain an England Under-21 cap.

Football League

Gary made his Football League debut for Bristol Rovers on December 16 1978 at Turf Moor, Burnley. He came on as a substitute for Peter Aitken in a 0-2 defeat for Rovers. The full

Bristol Rovers team that afteroon was: Thomas, Day, Aitken (Mabbutt), Harding, Taylor, Prince, Petts, Williams, Staniforth, Randall, Denehy.

On October 11 1980 Gary netted his first League goal for Rovers. It was his 55th League appearance for the club and came in a 1-3 defeat at Notts County. A week later he opened his home account in a 3-3 draw with Sheffield Wednesday, the only occasion that he scored in consecutive League games for Rovers.

He only once netted two goals in a League game for Rovers, that being on September 29 1981 in a 2-2 home draw with Wimbledon. The full list of League games in which Gary scored for Rovers is shown below:

11.10.80	v Notts County (A) – lost 1-3
18.10.80	v Sheffield Wednesday (H) – drew 3-3
4.11.80	v Watford (H) – won 3-1
27.12.80	v Luton Town (H) – lost 2-4
28. 3.81	v Preston North End (H) – won 2-0
29. 9.81	v Wimbledon (H) – drew 2-2
31.10.81	v Doncaster Rovers (A) – lost 2-4
30. 1.82	v Reading (H) – drew 1-1
20. 3.82	v Doncaster Rovers (H) – won 3-0

On May 10 1979 Gary was one of seven teenagers used by Rovers in their youngest-ever League team, at Wrexham. The total age of the twelve players used was 242, an average age of just over 20 per player. His final League match for Rovers was in a 2-1 win at Carlisle United, May 15 1982.

Following his transfer to Tottenham, Gary made his First Division debut on August 28 1982, when Luton Town were the visitors to White Hart Lane. He met Glenn Hoddle's third minute free kick with a firm header to register his first goal for the club. The Tottenham team in a 2-2 draw was; Clemence, Hughton, Miller, Lacy, Hazard, Perryman, Mabbutt, Archibald (Brooke), Galvin, Hoddle, Crooks.

Four weeks later – on September 25 – he scored his first of

two brace of goals for Tottenham. Nottingham Forest were the opponents at Tottenham for his first two-goal strike, and later that season, when Birmingham City were the visitors, he again achieved a double-score. In April 1983 and November 1985 Gary netted in consecutive League games for Spurs and the details of each match in which he has scored a League goal are as follows:

28. 8.82   v Luton Town (H) – drew 2-2
11. 9.82   v Manchester City (H) – lost 1-2
25. 9.82   v Nottingham Forest (H) – won 4-1
23.10.82   v Notts County (H) – won 4-2
18.12.82   v Birmingham City (H) – won 2-1
 9. 4.83   v Nottingham Forest (A) – drew 2-2
16. 4.83   v Ipswich Town (H) – won 3-1
 3. 5.83   v Southampton (A) – won 2-1
10. 9.83   v Leicester City (A) – won 3-0
18. 4.84   v Aston Villa (H) – won 2-1
17.11.84   v Ipswich Town (A) – won 3-0
26.12.84   v West Ham United (H) – drew 2-2
23.11.85   v Queens Park Rangers (H) – drew 1-1
30.11.85   v Aston Villa (A) – won 2-1
 8. 3.86   v West Bromwich Albion (H) – won 5-0
 7.12.86   v Manchester United (A) – drew 3-3
15. 8.87   v Coventry City (A) – lost 1-2
 4. 5.88   v Luton Town (H) – won 2-1
17.12.88   v West Ham United (A) – won 2-0

Gary's 57th minute goal at Old Trafford in December 1986 was Spurs' 3,500th in Division One of the Football League. He has played against 63 different clubs in the League, spread over the First, Second and Third Divisions, and he has faced only one club, Millwall, in all three Divisions.

Gary's 359 League appearances to date have come in 178 home games and 181 on opponents' grounds. Crystal Palace, Brighton and Hove Albion and Wolverhampton Wanderers have featured in his away matches, but not at home, while

Newport County were among home opponents but not away. Ironically, Gary would have created a personal best of 89 consecutive League matches for Bristol Rovers had he played at Newport County in March 1982. However, he was called up for his England Under-21 debut in Poland and missed that Third Division fixture!

FA Cup

Gary made his FA Cup debut at Swansea City on January 8 1979 in a 1-0 victory for Bristol Rovers. His fourth FA Cup match brought his first goal in the competition, at Preston a 4-3 victory. He has scored once in each of the four games listed below:

3.1.81   v Preston North End (A) – won 4-3
10.1.87 v Scunthorpe United (H) – won 3-2
31.1.87 v Crystal Palace (H) – won 4-0
16.5.87 v Coventry City (Wembley) – lost 2-3

Football League Cup
(incorporating the Milk and Littlewoods Cups)

Gary's League Cup debut was at Exeter City on August 9 1980 when Bristol Rovers gained a First Round First Leg 1-1 draw. His first goal came in the corresponding tie the following year, when a 1-1 draw was the result at Crewe Alexandra on September 2 1981 – his seventh appearance in the competition.

On November 6 1985 Gary netted his most recent goal in the competition in Spurs' 2-0 Third Round home win versus Wimbledon.

· GARY MABBUTT ·

European Competition

Coleraine of N Ireland provided the opposition for Gary's European debut. Played at their Showgrounds home on September 15 1982, the match, a European Cup-Winners' Cup First Round First Leg fixture, resulted in a 3-0 win for Tottenham. Gary was replaced by Mike Hazard in the 78th minute.

Thirteen days later in the Second Leg of the tie, Gary netted his first European goal, a 53rd minute strike from the edge of the penalty area. That was Spurs' second goal in a 4-0 win.

The following campaign in 1983-84 saw Gary play in nine of Spurs' 12 UEFA Cup matches which culminated in him gaining a winner's medal. His only other goals in Europe came during that season's First Round First Leg match at Drogheda, his goals – a 51st minute header and a spectacular 82nd minute shot – being the 4th and 6th in a 6-0 win.

European Competition by Club and Season

Club	TOTAL		1982–83		1983–84		1984–85	
	App	Gls	App	Gls	App	Gls	App	Gls
Anderlecht	2				2			
FK Austria Memphis	1				1			
Bayern Munich	2		2					
Bohemians Prague	2						2	
S.C. Braga	1						1	
F.C. Bruges	1						1	
Coleraine	2	1	2	1				
Drogheda	2	2			2	2		
Feyenoord	2				2			
Hajduk Split	2				2			

Football League appearances and goals by club and appearance

Club	TOTAL App	TOTAL Gls	1978-79 App	1978-79 Gls	1979-80 App	1979-80 Gls	1980-81 App	1980-81 Gls	1981-82 App	1981-82 Gls	1982-83 App	1982-83 Gls	1983-84 App	1983-84 Gls	1984-85 App	1984-85 Gls	1985-86 App	1985-86 Gls	1986-87 App	1986-87 Gls	1987-88 App	1987-88 Gls	1988-89 App	1988-89 Gls
Arsenal	12										2		1	1	1	1	2	2	2	2			2	2
Aston Villa	10	2									2		1	1	1	1	2	1			2			
Birmingham City	5	2									2	2	1				2							
Blackburn Rovers	2						2	2																
Bolton Wanderers	2						2	2																
Brentford	2								2															
Brighton & Hove Albion	1										1													
Bristol City	4						2		2															
Burnley	6	2	2		2	2																		
Cambridge United	4				2		2	2																
Cardiff City	5	1	1				2	2																
Carlisle United	2								2															
Charlton Athletic	7						2												1	2	2		2	
Chelsea	10				2	2									1		1							
Chester City	2								2	2														
Chesterfield	2								2	2														
Coventry City	11	1									2		1		1		1		2		2	1	2	
Crystal Palace	1		1																					
Derby County	6								2	2											2		2	
Doncaster Rovers	2	2							2	2														
Everton	10										1		2		1		1		1		2		2	
Exeter City	2								2	2														
Fulham	4	2			2		2																	
Gillingham	2								2															
Grimsby Town	2						2																	
Huddersfield Town	2						2						1	1										
Ipswich Town	5	2									2	1	1		1	1								

Team																		
Leicester City	8		1	1		2				2		1	1	1	1		2	2
Lincoln City	2								2		1						2	2
Liverpool	11	3		1		2	2		2	2	2	1	2	2	2	2	2	2
Luton Town	15	1	2	2	1	2	2		2	2	1	2	1	1	2	2	2	1
Manchester City	5	1		1		2	2	1	2	2	1		1	1	1	2	2	
Manchester United	12	1		1		2	2	1	2	2	2		1	1	2	2	1	
Middlesbrough	2					2												
Millwall	5	1	2		2	2				1					2	2		
Newcastle United	13	1	2	2		2	1		1				1	1		2	2	
Newport County	1					1										1		
Norwich City	11		2			2	2	2	1	2	1		2	2		2	2	2
Nottingham Forest	12	3	2	2	1	2	1	3	2	2	1		2	2		1	2	2
Notts County	7	2	1	2		2	2	1	2		1		2	1				
Oldham Athletic	3		2	2		2												
Orient	4																	
Oxford United	7			1		2					1		2			2	2	
Plymouth Argyle	2		2			2												
Portsmouth	4		2			2								2				
Preston North End	8	1	2	1		2	1		1				2	2		2	2	
Queens Park Rangers	14	1	2	2		2	1		2	2		1	2	2	2	2	2	2
Reading	2	1	2	1														
Sheffield Wednesday	12	1	2	2		2	2		2	2			2	2	2	2	2	2
Shrewsbury Town	4		2	2		2												
Southampton	9	1			1	1		1		1			2	2	1	1	1	
Southend United	2		2			2												
Stoke City	4								1	1			2	1		2		2
Sunderland	5		2	2			2		2		1							
Swansea City	5		2			2			2									
Swindon Town	2		1						2									
Walsall	2			2		2												
Watford	12	1	2	2	1	2	1		2	2	1		2	1	1	2	2	2
West Bromwich Albion	7	1		1		2	1		2	2	2		1	1				
West Ham United	12	2	2	2	1	1	1		1	1	1	1	1	1	2	2	2	2
Wimbledon	7	2			2			2		1			2					
Wolverhampton Wanderers	1								1									1
Wrexham	4	1	1		2					1			2					

Summary of Club Appearances

Season	Football League App	Gls	F.A. Cup App	Gls	League Cup App	Gls	European Competition App	Gls	Charity Shield App	Gls	Super Cup App	Gls	TOTAL App	Gls
1978-79	11^3		2^1										13	
1979-80	33^6	5	1										34	6
1980-81	42	5	2	1	6								50	6
1981-82	45		1		4	1							50	
Bristol R.	131	10	6	1	10	1							147	12
1982-83	38	10	3^1		5		4	1	1				51	11
1983-84	21	2	2		2		9^2	2					34	4
1984-85	25^{10}	2	2^1		4^2		4^1						35	2
1985-86	32^3	3	5		5	1					6^1		48	4
1986-87	37	1	6	3	8								51	4
1987-88	37	2	2		3								42	2
1988-89	38	1	1		5								44	1
Tottenham	228	21	21	3	32	1	17	3	1		6		305	28
Total	359	31	27	4	42	2	17	3	1		6		452	40

Superior figures show substitute appearances included in appearance figure.

F.A. Cup by Club and Season

Club	TOTAL		1978-79		1979-80		1980-81		1981-82		1982-83		1983-84		1984-85		1985-86		1986-87		1987-88		1988-89	
	App	Gls	App	Gls	App	Gls	App	Gls	App	Gls	App	Gls	App	Gls	App	Gls	App	Gls	App	Gls	App	Gls	App	Gls
Aston Villa	1				1																			
Bradford City	1																						1	
Charlton Athletic	2		1												1									
Coventry City	1	1																	1	1				
Crystal Palace	1	1																	1	1				
Everton	2										1				1									
Fulham	1								1															
Liverpool	1														1									
Newcastle United	1																1							
Norwich City	2												2											
Notts County	2																2							
Oldham Athletic	1																1							
Oxford United	2																				2			
Port Vale	1																				1			
Preston North End	1	1					1	1																
Scunthorpe United	1	1																	1	1				
Southampton	2						1				1													
Swansea City	1		1																					
Watford	1																1							
West Bromwich Albion	1										1													
Wimbledon	1																1							

Football League Cup by Club and Season

Club	TOTAL		1980–81		1981–82		1982–83		1983–84		1984–85		1985–86		1986–87		1987–88		1988–89	
	App	Gls	App	Gls	App	Gls	App	Gls	App	Gls	App	Gls	App	Gls	App	Gls	App	Gls	App	Gls
Arsenal	3														3					
Aston Villa	1																1			
Barnsley	1														1					
Birmingham City	1														1					
Blackburn Rovers	2																		2	
Brighton & Hove Albion	2						2													
Burnley	1						1													
Cambridge United	1														1					
Crewe Alexandra	2	1			2	1														
Exeter City	2		2																	
Gillingham	1						1													
Halifax Town	2										2									
Lincoln City	2								2											
Luton Town	1						1													
Northampton Town	2				2															
Notts County	2																		2	
Orient	1												1							
Portsmouth	5		2										3							
Southampton	1																		1	
Sunderland	2										2									
Torquay United	2																2			
West Ham United	2														2					
Wimbledon	1	1											1	1						
York City	2		2